DATA SCIENCE FOR
SUICIDE BOMBINGS

DATA SCIENCE FOR SUICIDE BOMBINGS

CAN YOU PREDICT THE NEXT ATTACK?

SANA RASHEED

iUniverse

DATA SCIENCE FOR SUICIDE BOMBINGS
CAN YOU PREDICT THE NEXT ATTACK?

iUniverse books may be ordered through booksellers or by contacting:

iUniverse
1663 Liberty Drive
Bloomington, IN 47403
www.iuniverse.com
1-800-Authors (1-800-288-4677)

Because of the dynamic nature of the Internet, any web addresses or links contained in this book may have changed since publication and may no longer be valid. The views expressed in this work are solely those of the author and do not necessarily reflect the views of the publisher, and the publisher hereby disclaims any responsibility for them.

Any people depicted in stock imagery provided by Thinkstock are models, and such images are being used for illustrative purposes only. Certain stock imagery © Thinkstock.

ISBN: 978-1-5320-1296-9 (sc)
ISBN: 978-1-5320-1297-6 (e)

Library of Congress Control Number: 2016920247

Print information available on the last page.

iUniverse rev. date: 12/13/2016

Preface

Suicide bombing has become one of the most lethal and favorite modus operandi of terrorist organizations around the world. Pakistan has faced a total of 488 suicide attacks in last decade; that resulted in 7,227 deaths and 15,326 injuries. On average, there were at least one casualty and four injuries each day in suicide bombing attacks during same time period. Information technology and artificial intelligence have seen some tremendous advancement in recent years and this study is set to use the power of data sciences and predictive analytics for counter-terrorism and suicide bombings. This multidisciplinary research work has not only outlined a theoretical framework for personal traumatization, but also discusses the methods and ways to analyze the data to uncover trends and patterns, and examined the use of statistical models that could help in forecasting suicide bombings. The factual cause of suicide bombers is revenge against the powerful enemy. When the struggle between humans for survival becomes so heightened that people were compelled to compete with each other for power in society, then hatred starts to emerge between them that can lead towards the harsh decisions. Personal traumatic events can cause people to become violent. Terrorist organizations take advantage of such people and motivate them by exploiting their feelings. For statistical analysis, new database has been formulated to cover all possible factors which could be identified from the news. During the statistical analysis, the hypothesized statement has been nullified. Suicide bombing proliferated in 2007; and in the same year, the incident of Lal Masjid and the formulation of Tehreek–e-Taliban Pakistan (TTP) took place. The

TTP is the largest militant group in Pakistan, and it is originated in Khyber Pakhtunkha (KPK). The province of KPK is the highly targeted province. The cities, Peshawar and Quetta are the top victims of suicide attacks and the only commonality between both cities is, the pathway of NATO supply to Afghanistan. Further, it has been identified that the TTP and Lashkar-e-Jhangvi (LeJ) are most likely to attack on Thursday and Friday; while Sunday and Tuesday are least preferred by them. LeJ executed the only sectarian attack and killed twice the number of people per attack than TTP. Conditional Inferential Tree algorithm has been used as a prediction model. It has been trained on the scenario and cross validated on 3 factors of suicide attacks. An accuracy rate of over 70% has been achieved.

Acknowledgments

In the name of Allah, the most beneficent and the most merciful, to Him is due all praise. I thank my Allah S.W.T. for enabling me to accomplish this research and put this work together.

> "If the only prayer you ever say in your entire life is 'thank you', it will be enough."
>
> ~Meister Eckhart

Words alone cannot adequately express my sincere gratitude to all those who helped me during the development of this research work. I am indebted to many people who provided remarkable help to explore, formulate, understand, and perform the statistical analysis on the dataset of suicide bombing. Some are more important than others because they helped me at the right time, at the right place, and with the right kind of guidance.

My special gratitude to my mother Anjum-un-Nisa, father Abdul Rasheed and brother Muhammad Shoaib. I am grateful to Dr. Khuram Iqbal for his research advising. I am glad to be his student. I would also like to thank Dr. Zeeshan-ul-hassan Usmani for his support and co-operation and for having a confidence in my inter-disciplinary pursuit.

Special thanks to my fellows and colleagues who helped me whenever I was stuck, to my friend Nabia Mansoor for always be a push for me, to Major Rashidullah Khan for helping me in semester courses, to Adnan Khalid for helping me with statistics, to Anum Aquil who helped me in data maintenance, to my dearest cousin Ateeqa Masood for her continuous prayers, special thanks to Kulsum Abbasi for proof reading and of course to Aqsa Malik and Syyab bin Abdul Khaliq Rahi.

Thank you my Raab and thank you all very much.

Sana Rasheed
sana-rasheed@outlook.com

1. Introduction

Suicide terrorism is the most dreadful challenge for Pakistan because the country has been one of its prime targets during recent years. Approximately 3,021 Pakistanis were killed in terrorist attacks in 2009, a figure that was 33 percent higher than in 2008. In the recent accumulated figure of causalities, 6,524 people have been killed in 450 suicide attacks in Pakistan and 16,527 had been injured.[1] Overall, the casualty rate is very high and has drastically been affecting Pakistan's progress at a large scale.

Constitutionally, Pakistan is an Islamic Republic State, which got its independence in August 1947. It started its journey of socio-economic and political development, according to the vision of its creator – Quaid-e-Azam Muhammad Ali Jinnah. Although Pakistan faced countless vicissitudes, political instability, and numerous problems, it quickly emerged as a strong country. Pakistan's society was renowned as the most peaceful in terms of social violence and suicide terrorism. Neither was any sectarian or ethnic dispute outstretched and publicized with negative objectives, nor was the society driven to hopelessness or retaliation on these concerns. However, ever since the Russian invasion of Afghanistan in 1979, the society experienced a significant twist in the social fabric and politico-economic system. At the time of the Soviet invasion of Afghanistan in 1979, Pakistan worked with the United States to help support the Afghan insurgency. Both countries aided the Jihadi group under the label of *Mujahedeen*. After defeating the Soviets through *Mujahedeen*, the United States abandoned the region and imposed economic sanctions, known as the Pressler Amendment, on Pakistan in 1990 because of its nuclear weapon program.[2] On the other hand, political instability, corruption, social injustice and economic imbalance gave rise to different forms of terrorism. We now classify it as a negative peace. The political situation in Pakistan had changed considerably. In this changed scenario, terrorism holds a tight grasp and continues to spread swiftly.

Prior to the Pressler Amendment, the United States had invested $1.2 billion on military equipment for the demise of the Soviet Union. It was a country specific law that knocks out only one nation on the nuclear issue.[3] It has been presumed that the Pressler sanctions were applied when Pakistan's co-operation was no longer needed. As a result, an air of contention propagated between them and deeply intensified after the incident of 9/11. The U.S. initiated its War on Terror project and asked Pakistan for help. The 9/11 incident actually helped the U.S. to return to the region. The United States then applied tactics of pressure to compel Pakistan to provide its soil and resources to United States for an invasion of Afghanistan and also an indirect invasion of Pakistan. Gen. Pervez Musharraf was the President of Pakistan and he took a stand with the U.S. on this issue. This, in turn, created the image of Pakistan as a client state of the United States and inevitably injected a feeling of rebellion in the people of Pakistan, especially in the northern areas of Pakistan, where people have a closer affiliation with Afghanistan on the basis of religious equivalent. The extremist groups, thus, went on the path of insurgency. This, briefly, was how the phenomenon of terrorism transpired in Pakistan and impaired the society in various ways.

1.1. Motivation and Background

This analysis of suicide attacks in Pakistan was conducted in the context of a continuous increase in attacks after the Lal Masjid operation in July 2007.[4] These attacks witnessed a sharp rise after 2007, and this trend persisted till 2010. Since the first attack of this kind took place in 1995, there occurred a total of 42 suicide attacks in Pakistan before the Lal Masjid operation. After the operation, 47 suicide attacks were counted in major cities of Pakistan in just the remaining six months of 2007. Since then, 256 suicide attacks have been recorded nation-wide in Pakistan[5] over the next three years. Therefore, 100 percent more suicide attacks were carried out in the reaction of General Pervez Musharraf's military government policies. He had succumbed to pressure from the international community to prevent the use of Pakistani territory as a sanctuary for Al Qaeda and Taliban. After the Operation of *Rah-e-Nijat* (the Path to Salvation) by the military forces in FATA in 2009, a sharp increase in suicide attacks was again noted. 77 attacks were recorded in this year alone, as compared to the previous years.[6] It cannot conclusively be said that the occupation of a country leads to suicide attacks, but the fact is that due to the presence of US and NATO forces in Afghanistan, Pakistan has been a prime target of suicide attacks. This is also true for other Muslim countries such as Saudi Arabia, which has experienced multiple suicide attacks by Al-Qaeda because of Riyadh's policy in favor of US in the war on terrorism. One of the first attempts of suicide attacks in Pakistan started after 9/11 when Pakistan chose to act against Taliban and Al Qaeda in support of the U.S. This first incident of suicide attack in Pakistan was carried out in 2002 in Karachi against French Engineers.[7]

In the domain of suicide terrorism, previous research has discussed the factors and root causes of suicide bombing so far. They underlined the reasons behind suicide terrorism in the perspective of social violence, personal traumatization and deprivation, humiliation, revenge, and vengance, etc. All the studies were interlinked with psychology, and their focus was to develop psychological profiles of suicide bombers. Researchers also focused on elucidating the strategic and political gains of suicide bombing and their role in destabilizing countries. No work, however, has been done so far in the domain of statistical analysis and predictive modeling on the case study of suicide bombing in Pakistan. There is also an enormous amount of data present on suicide terrorism and primarily maintained by international organizations, but their counts can be doubtful and not of much help when measuring the accuracy of attacks and casualties.

With the current knowledge about data and statistics; and recent advances in predictive analytics along with the help of the emerging field of data science, one should be able to create and analyze a statistical model to identify the hidden pattern and predict the future trends of the phenomenon. The data analysis with statistical models can assist in making recommendations to public policies and decision-making.

The goal of the thesis is to map the social sciences phenomena – suicide bombing, with statistical analysis to explore the hidden information from data and to identify how statistical models can help in predicting the attacks. To achieve these goals, the formulation of a new database on the counts and details of each suicide attack is needed. Chapter 3 of this thesis presents the study of existing databases, the data collection and the formulation of a new database in support of these goals.

This multidisciplinary research touches the domains of Social Science (to cross test the existing explanations), Statistics (advance sampling models), Data Engineering (to build up architecture to analyze and process the data), Data Analysis (to perform exploratory data analysis to find hidden patterns), Data Visualization (to demonstrate graphs in a lucid way), and Predictive Analytics (models use for prediction). This research work has numerous applications and advancements that can be lent to any social phenomenon.

1.2. Research Questions

The key question that arises and will addressed in the study is:

1. How statistical modeling can help in the forecasting of emerging trends and patterns of suicide terrorism in Pakistan?
2. How the concept of suicide terrorism evolved?

3. Which international organizations are monitoring the incidents of suicide attacks in Pakistan?
4. What is the importance of maintaining suicide terrorism database and which features are important to record on suicide attacks?

1.3. Hypothesis

There is a strong correlation between suicide bombing and drone attacks in Pakistan.

1.4. Research Scope and Objectives

The main objectives of the thesis are to find the statistical correlation between suicide bombing and drone attacks in Pakistan and to provide an overview of how statistical models can help in forecasting. By identifying the models, it is likely to establish a more comprehensive understanding of ways to make use of advance statistical models to find existing patterns from data and to predict suicide attacks, or any social phenomenon, for that matter. The goals of this research are:

1. To formulate a comprehensive dataset of suicide bombing in Pakistan
2. To analyze the dataset to find useful insights about suicide attacks
3. To explore the statistical models that can help in forecasting

The predictive model has benchmarked by the cross-validation process on three data split sets. The R programming language[8], RStudio[9], and Microsoft Excel tools have been used to perform data analysis and advanced statistical analysis.

1.5.   Limitations of the Study

This research is restricted to advanced statistical models. In such models, there are two extended domains, data mining and machine learning, which provide a wide range of such algorithms (a self-contained step-by-step set of operations to be performed) that can be implemented to any given social phenomena that can learn from history and predict future trends.

1.6.   Theoretical Framework and Methodology

This is a multidisciplinary research that cross tests the issue in the theoretical frameworks of vengeance, and personal traumatization and deprivation; and explores the quantitative statistical analysis for social sciences. Quantitative statistics has been widely used in the domain of social science. It is comprised with literature review, the history of evolution of suicide bombing and its analysis.

This study is focused largely towards the quantitative analysis of suicide bombing in Pakistan in order to recognize the existing hidden patterns. The mixed research methodology has applied by using qualitative and quantitative research inductive approach. This study also uses a mix of descriptive, research and casual comparative research methods. Secondary data has been consulted to formulate a complete database for the analysis of suicide bombing.

1.7.   Organization of the Book

The book is divided into the following chapters: Chapter 1 discusses the existing theories that can be applied to the phenomenon of suicide bombing. Chapter 2 describes the development of the concept of suicide bombing and how it evolved in Pakistan. Chapter 3 explores the existing datasets on suicide bombing in Pakistan and discusses the formulation of a new and detailed dataset of suicide bombing. Chapter 4 performs the data analysis of suicide bombing and extends to find the correlation with drone attacks. Chapter 5 explores advance statistical models which help in prediction and also convey the accuracy of results. The thesis concludes with a research summary and future directions.

Notes

1 "Suicide Bombing", Pakistan Body Count, http://www.pakistanbodycount.org/bla.php.

2 "Context of August 1985: Pressler Amendment Passed, Requiring Yearly Certification that Pakistan Does Not Have Nuclear Weapons," History Commons,

3 "The Pakistan - US Relationship," Geo-Political Affairs, Defence Journal, http://www.defencejournal.com/april98/pakistanus.htm.

4 Qudsia Akhlaque, "Its Operation Sunrise, not Silence," Dawn, July 11, 2007, accessed on Aug 25, 2014, http://www.dawn.com/2007/07/12/top7.htm

5 Pakistan Body Count, Year-wise distribution is 2002 (2 attacks), 2003 (2), 2004 (8), 2005 (4), 2006 (9), 2007 (57), 2008 (61), 2009 (90) and 2010 (58).

6 Khuram Iqbal, "Strategic measures to counter suicide terrorism in Pakistan," Pakistan Institute for Peace Studies Report, February 15, 2010, accessed August 25, 2014, http://san-pips.com/index.php?action=ra&id=pvt_list_1

7 "Suicide bombing leaves 14 dead: Explosive-laden car blows up near bus outside hotel," *Dawn*, May 09, 2002, accessed on Aug 25, 2014, http://archives.dawn.com/2002/05/09/top1.htm

8 W. N. Venables, D. M. Smith and the R Core Team, "An Introduction to R," accessed July 1, 2015, http://cran.r-project.org/doc/manuals/R-intro.pdf.

9 RStudio, https://www.rstudio.com/.

2. Theoretical Framework

The psychology of suicide bombing is unique because it requires an incredibly high level of commitment. Suicide bombing is a phenomenon where an individual personally deploys explosives and detonates it to perpetrate the greatest conceivable damage, killing himself or herself in the process. Suicide attackers are made, not born. The pertinent question remains, what motivates people to sacrifice his/her identity that will end in a process that causes irreversible and irreparable damage? Why are individuals willing to adopt the identity of a religious warrior that has no connection to humanity and is destined for premature death under the most critical circumstances? Many scholars have answered questions like these. Factors that motivate people towards suicide bombing are very significant for any terrorist organization. They use them as a weapon to achieve their objectives. Suicide terrorism is a terrorist tactic aimed at achieving broader political goals in the society.[1] The real objective of these suicide attacks is to gain the attention of the population, government and worldwide media. Suicide bombing is shocking on account of the fact that the killing is indiscriminate in nature, and is apparently intended to kill or injure anyone within range because of the evident willingness of the bombers to die by their own hands, Usually, the victims are unsuspecting civilians - frequently, military personnel and political figures are the prime targets[2]

It is generally assumed that three things are necessary for a crime to be committed: a motivated offender, a suitable target, and the lack of a capable guardian. In the counterterrorism realm, similar principles apply. At the bare minimum, there are three main requirements for a suicide attack: (1) suicidal intent, (2) access to weapons, and (3) access to enemy targets. If these three factors are present, a suicide attack can be launched.[3]

There are some additional facilitators of suicide terrorism attacks and prolonged suicide terrorism campaigns. These include (4) homicidal intent, (5) a sponsoring terrorist organization, (6) social approval of suicide terrorism, and (7) social stigma of conventional suicide.[4]

Jeffrey William Lewis, describe the Mechanizing Humans in the perspective of suicide bombing. Suicide bombing integrates people with material devices to create a weapon both inexpensive and intelligent. Throughout history, human beings have been used as components of economic and technological systems by other humans.[5]

"Not only human physical labor, but also mental labor, can be exploited in technological systems. By the late 1800s, people were used as data processors within extremely sophisticated computational systems. By the Second World War, human and machine elements were integrated into hybrid control systems in which both human and machine were engineered and modified to improve system performance." [6]

Therefore, suicide bombing draws upon a long history of the human use of other human beings as the data processing centers in technological systems.[7]

The real goal of terrorism is to create intolerance, fear among the members of society and disturb the social, political and economic pattern. To understand the meaning of terrorism, it is important to look at the word 'violence', which is strongly related to the word terrorism. The term violence is derived from Latin "violaer" that means to violate or to go against those norms and values that are accepted by the members of the society or to misuse them. Similarly, terrorism means to impose one's perception of religious teachings, socio-cultural, and politico-economic values and norms by creating violence in the society.[8]

A suicide attack is a violent attack in which the attacker blows himself/ herself up with the intention to kill others or cause great destruction and expects to die in the process. They attach explosives bombs to their bodies or vehicles, which permits them to access crowded areas where placing explosives would otherwise be difficult.[9]

Having defined the key concepts, the following section summarizes some of the existing theories put forth by the scholars of counter-terrorism.

2.1. Vengeance

Brook, Pedahzur, and Hassan[10] argue that revenge, including individual retaliation, is one acclaimed reason for someone to be motivated to become a suicide bomber. According to Pedahzur, a study was conducted on 180 suicide bombers and the researchers found that approximately half of individuals who went on suicide missions had recently lost a friend or family member or other significant person in their lives. Sheikh Ahmad Yassin, the former leader of Hamas, explains that revenge is deeply embedded in the Muslim culture, and he stated that "in response to any action by the Israelis, I take my revenge... I pay you back, an eye for an eye, a tooth for a tooth". At the same time, there are many other factors that lead suicide bombers to make such decisions. The motivational factors can be based on ideology and religion, in addition to vengeance. Ariel Merari[11] conducted a study of 34 Palestinian suicide attacks and suggests, based on interviews with the suicide attacker's family, that the organizations claimed the attacks as revenge for Israeli retaliation; it was not based on the attacker's personal revenge.

Dr. Adrian Mirvish, a professor of philosophy, has described the suicide bomber as one with just a shell around an empty mind.

> *"In the case of suicide bomber, we are in effect dealing with a strange case of inverted solipsism... The authoritarian structure if the Islamic organizations... molds and shapes an inverted personage, one where there is no internal life left over, In place of a private mind and ground for conscience there is instead a rigid set of prescriptions totally open to public scrutiny. Better yet, through years of enforcement of hatred one is left with the mere shell of a complete person, one where the mind is merely a mirror, the product of absolute, authoritarian and public scrutiny"* [12]

Considering the point of view of scientific Western psychology, it is believed that any act we commit to damage our lives, and the lives of others needs to be perceived as unhealthy. The motivational factors can be based on ideology, religion, or vengeance.

Charny, I. W. emphasized the psychology of a suicide attacker. People who kill themselves and kill other people should certainly not be thought of as mentally healthy.[13] There are many factors that lead them to make such decisions. The motivational factors are complex to understand: "humiliation, revenge, and altruism" all drive the individual to engage in, and the community to condone, suicide bombing. Participating in suicide bombing can fulfill a range of interpretations from "personal to communal".[14] They see life from a different perspective in which the sense of being superior after death by killing others win them over. They are suffering from weakness of mind in which they are unable to accept reality. They are dehumanized during training by the terrorist organization. Such organizations manipulate them on the basis of ideology and religion in such a way that their beliefs become weak and they are obligated to start viewing things from an unrealistic prospective. These unrealities lead them to take the lives of others by sacrificing their lives, however, in reality this act is far from a 'sacrifice'.

Riaz Hassan also underlined that sometimes people react unreasonably when they perceive injustice, and the dark side of their mind motivates them to take revenge. He described revenge as "a response to continuous suffering of an aggrieved community. At the heart of the whole process are perceptions of personal harm, unfairness and injustice, along with anger, indignation, and hatred associated with such perceptions."[15] Such thoughts lead them to take the lives of others through suicide terrorism.

Noam Shpance highlighted another psychological aspect, which he terms "true believerism", and holds that the destructive force is derived from the process, rather than from content. Once the 'true believing' process is in place, it can be transferred to any content, and will produce similarly destructive results. For example, the true believers of Israel and Palestine differ significantly on content but process-wise they are similar: brutal and aggressive to each other and willing to give their lives for it.[16] The real cause of suicide bombers is revenge against the powerful enemy. When the struggle between humans for survival becomes so heightened that people were compelled to compete with each other for power in society, then hatred starts to emerge between them that can lead towards the harsh decisions. People in such societies are instilled with immense hate and anger, which motivate them to take revenge for their satisfaction and for that they decide upon the course of suicide attacks.

2.2. Personal Traumatization and Deprivation

Some scholars believe that suicide bombers are motivated by personal traumatization.[17] Deep grief and personal traumatization[18] can be a prompt for a potential suicide bomber. Such traumatization can emerge from the conditions under which most Palestinians live (unemployment, Israeli checkpoints, and incarceration), and can also be a result of the vivid images of injustice enacted on their fellow Palestinians witnessed through the media. On the other hand, Hafez[19] opposes this viewpoint, saying that traumatization does not fully explain why someone chose to become suicide bomber. He states that even though traumatic events can cause people to become violent; this violence could manifest itself in other ways instead. Other authors, like Mia Bloom and Robert

A. Pape agree that explanations such as the limitation of economic opportunities, low social status, or mental syndromes, such as not having a hold on reality.[20][21] Brym and Araj reported that no evidence exists to support a deprivation theory.[22]

Eamon Murphy highlighted one of the root causes of suicide attacks and cited personal traumatization and deprivation as factors that lead people to go for suicide attacks.[23] Sometimes disastrous events lead people to become violent, when they lose all hope and when they feel that their life has become meaningless. The state of traumatization does not let someone differentiate between right or wrong, and the mind starts to behave violently. Terrorist organizations take advantage of such people and motivate them by exploiting their feelings. The writer here gave an example of an 18-year-old boy who committed a suicide attack to take revenge of his sister's death. Suicide attacks are very difficult to prevent because it is a clandestine activity that is committed by the people who get themselves involved in the community. They mingle in society, adopting the homogenous culture of the society, which makes it impossible to exclude them. The society is unable to differentiate and identify them as the enemy.

Furthermore, suicide terrorism has no connection with a specific religion, region or culture. Mostly, such attacks and their perpetrators were used in political armed conflicts. In the book *Dying to Win*, Robert Pape concluded that the taproot of suicide terrorism is nationalism. There is an insufficient connection between suicide terrorism and Islamic fundamentalism, or with any other religion in the world. However, what all suicide terrorist attacks have in common is that they are a specific secular and strategic goal: to coerce modern democracies to withdraw military forces from the territory that the terrorists consider to be their homeland.[24] He argues that suicide terrorism is "an extreme strategy for national liberation".[25] Papes extended his research work with Feldman in Cutting the Fuse and evaluating more than 2100 suicide attacks, conducting detailed case studies of the eight largest campaigns and offered extended policy recommendations.

Professor Riaz Hassan states that the conventional wisdom that bombers are insane or religious fanatics is misplaced. Bombers show no personality disorders. Attacks are often politically motivated, aimed at achieving specific strategic goals, such as forcing concessions or generating greater support. Rosemarie Skanie also highlighted some of the factors of the terrorist's extremist perception about the sects of the religion. One of the primary tactics they use to fulfill their objective of spreading violence is to spark sectarian clash.

Hence, the reasons of suicide bombing are highly dependent on the factors behind them. Factors that motivate the attacker could vary and the objectives of terrorist organizations are also multifarious. The researcher has analyzed the suicide terrorism issue in the perspective of vengeance and personal traumatization and deprivation theories.

As this research is multidisciplinary, the domain of Quantitative analysis (a branch of statistics) has been discussed here in the perspective of social science, in order to provide an overview of how statistical models can help in identifying hidden information from data and in forecasting.

2.3. Quantitative Social Sciences

Statistics is a branch of mathematical science that involves the collection, analysis and interpretation of data. Statistics deals with both qualitative and quantitative types of data. Various specialties[26] have advanced and yet advanced statistical theory and methods continue to be applied to various disciplines. In the field of social sciences, statistics formulated as a new term called Social Statistics. Social scientists can use statistics for various purposes, including analyzing behaviors of groups of people in their environment and special situations, and determining people's needs through statistical sampling.[27] Statistics has been widely used in the field of social sciences. Harvard University, for example, has developed institutes that are focusing on "quantitative social science."[28] The researcher will analyze the suicide bombing issue in the context of the stated purposes, focusing on quantitative analysis.

In quantitative social science, multilevel models, factor analysis and cluster analysis are a few of the widely used statistically techniques.

2.3.1. Multilevel models

Multilevel modeling is a generalized form of linear regression methods, which can also extend to non-linear models. Linear models are used to study how a quantitative variable depends on one or more predictors or explanatory variables. The predictors themselves may be quantitative or qualitative.[29] They facilitate the understanding and prediction of the behavior of complex systems and help analyze data. Nonlinear models are those models where the relationship between dependent and independent variables is nonlinear. Multilevel models recognize the existence of such data hierarchies by allowing for residual components at each level in the hierarchy.

To take an example, a simple linear regression model might predict that a given randomly sampled person in Seattle (a city of Washington) would have an average yearly income $10,000 higher than an equivalent person in Mobile, Alabama. However, it would also predict, for example, that a white person might have an average income $7,000 above a black person, and a 65-year-old might have an income $3,000 below a 45-year-old, in both cases regardless of location. A multilevel model, however, would allow for different regression coefficients for each predictor in each location.[30] Multilevel models can be used on data with many levels, although 2-level models are the most common. The dependent variable must be examined at the lowest level of analysis.[31] It can be used in prediction, data reduction and causal inference for observational and experiments studies.

2.3.2.　Factor Analysis

Factor analysis is a statistical method used to describe variability among observed, correlated variables in terms of a potentially lower number of unobserved variables called factors.[32] For example, people may respond similarly to questions about education, occupation, and income, which are all associated with unobserved variable socioeconomic status. Usually, it is used in applied sciences that deal with large quantities of data. Factor analysis has two further types and various additional types to compute factoring.

2.3.3.　Cluster Analysis

Cluster analysis is one of the exploratory data analysis tools that aims to sort different objects into groups in a way that the degree of association between two objects is maximal if they belong to the same group and minimal otherwise.[33] Briefly, it is a technique to group the objects of a similar kind into respective categories. For example, a group of guests sharing the same table in a restaurant can be considered to be a cluster of people. Another example is, items of the similar nature at food stores, such as different types of meat or vegetables are arranged in the same or nearby locations.[34] Whenever we need to organize a "mountain" of information into manageable, meaningful piles, cluster analysis is of great utility.[35] Several clustering algorithms lie under the umbrella of cluster analysis.

In the domain of quantitative social sciences, RAND Corporation conducted an extensive research with the title *Predicting Suicide Bombing*. The threat of suicide bombings provoked the Department of Homeland Security to mandate the Naval Research Laboratory (NRL) to develop such methods, which helps in predicting the determinants of suicide bombing attacks.[36] They choose four Israeli cities to study suicide bombings: Jerusalem, Haifa, Tel Aviv, and Netanya during and after the Second Intifada (1993–2006). They collected data from Israeli

Central Bureau of Statistics, which they refer to as "neighborhoods."[37] In the quantitative analysis section, they genuinely focused on the sociocultural, socioeconomic, demographic, and political aspects of the suicide bomber attacks. They used five categories of data for analysis.

Socioeconomic Characteristics: The Israeli Central Bureau of Statistics collects multiple socioeconomic indicators i.e. unemployment, housing density, average income, etc. for every neighborhood in Israel.

Demographic Characteristics: Targets of the suicide bombing people or infrastructure, religious, racial-ethnic, and other demographic features.

Electoral Data: obtained 1999 voting data for the Knesset by polling station and aggregated the data to the neighborhood level.

Proximity to the terrorist safe house: collected coordinates for all known Palestinian Islamic Jihad, Hamas, and Al-Aqsa terrorist safe houses in the region.

Socio-cultural Precipitants: They compiled a list of precipitants that have been theorized to be associated with the timing of suicide bombing attacks. Existing research has identified religious holidays, political events, and other occurrences as potential precipitants that trigger suicide bombing attacks. Martyrdom videos made by suicide bombers have explicitly referred to political negotiations and high-profile meetings, such as the Arab League Summit.

They performed data analysis in R language (a programming language use to perform statistical analysis). Principal Component Analysis, Classification and Regression Trees, and Logistic Regression Model (types of Multilevel Models) were used for analysis and compared their results with NRL Risk Index Regression Results.

The researcher will be utilizing the Conditional Inference Tree in advance statistical analysis. This technique covers the Multilevel Models and Factor Analysis with the combination of Conditional Probability and Decision Tress. Conditional Probability lies under the domain of Probability Theory,[38] and Decision Tree lies under Data Mining.[39] She will be using R[40][41], RStudio[42], and Microsoft Excel – as tools to perform data analysis and advanced statistical analysis.

Notes

1   Robert A. Pape, *Dying to Win: The Strategic Logic of Suicide Terrorism* (New York: Random House, 2005).

2   James Kiras, "Suicide Bombing," Encyclopedia Britannica, Aug 07, 2014, accessed May 9, 2015, http://www.britannica.com/EBchecked/topic/736115/suicide-bombing.

3   Adam Lankford, "Requirements and Facilitators for Suicide Terrorism: an Explanatory Framework for Prediction and Prevention," *Perspective on Terrorism* 5, no. 5-6 (2011), accessed May 21, 2015, http://www.terrorismanalysts.com/pt/index.php/pot/article/view/requirements-and-facilitators/html.

4   Ibid.

5   Jeffrey William Lewis, "The Human Use of Human Beings: A Brief History of Suicide Bombing," *Origins - Current Events in Historical Perspective* 6, no. 7, 2013.

6   Ibid.

7   Ibid.

8   Sabir Michael, "Terrorism a Socio-Economic and Political Phenomenon with Special Reference to Pakistan", *Journal of Management and Social Sciences* 3, no. 1, (Spring 2007), p. 36

9   Amy Zalman, "Suicide Bomber", About News, accessed May 27, 2015, http://terrorism.about.com/od/tacticsandweapons/g/SuicideBomber.htm.

10 Riaz Hassan, "What motivated the suicide bombers?," *Yale Global Online Magazine*, September 3, 2009, accessed August 21, 2014, http://yaleglobal.yale.edu/print/5926.

11 Ariel Merari, *Driven to death: Psychological and social aspects of suicide terrorism*, (New York: Oxford University Press, Inc., 2010)

12 Adrian Mirvish (2001), Suicide bombers, authoritarian minds, and the denial of others, quotation on pp. 7 and 5 of Internet reprinting. Mirvish is described as a Professor of Philosophy at California State University at Chico, who writes on Sartre and existential psychoanalysis.

13 I. W. Charny, *Fighting suicide bombing: A Worldwide campaign for* life (Connecticut: Praeger Security International, 2007), p. 94.

14 Riaz Hassan, "What Motivates the Suicide Bombers?", Yale Center for the Study of Globalization (2009), accessed May 12, 2015, http://yaleglobal.yale.edu/content/what-motivates-suicide-bombers-0

15 Riaz Hassan, "What motivates the Suicide Bombers?," Yale Globa;, September 3, 2009, accessed February 17, 2015, http://yaleglobal.yale.edu/content/what-motivates-suicide-bombers-0.

16 Noam Shpancer, "Understanding the Suicide Bomber", Psychology Today, Sep 32, 2010, accessed March 10, 2015, https://www.psychologytoday.com/blog/insight-therapy/201009/understanding-the-suicide-bomber

17 Anne Speckhard, "Understanding suicide terrorism Countering human bombs and their senders", *Fighting Terrorism in the Liberal State* 9, (2005): 158 - 175

18 Ibid: p. 4.

19 Muhammad Hafez, "Manufacturing human bombs the making of Palestinian suicide bombers", Washington D.C, United States: Institute of Peace. (2006)

20 Mia Bloom, *Dying to Kill: The Allure of Suicide* Terror (NY: Columbia University Press 2005)

21 Robert A. Pape, *Dying to Win: The Strategic Logic of Suicide Terrorism* (New York: Random House, 2005),

22 Brym & Araj, "Suicide bombing as strategy and interaction: The case of the second intifada", Social Forces. 84 no. 4, (2006): 1971.

23 Eamon Murphy, *The Making of Terrorism in Pakistan: Historical and Social Roots of Extremism* (Oxon and New York: Routledge Critical Terrorism Studies, 2013).

24 Robert A. Pape, *Dying to Win: The Strategic Logic of Suicide Terrorism* (New York: Random House, 2005), p. 4.

25 Ibid. 79-80.

26 "List of fields of application of statistics", Wikipedia, accessed May 19, 2015, http://en.wikipedia.org/wiki/List_of_fields_of_application_of_statistics

27 "Social Statistics," Wikipedia, accessed 19 May, 2015, http://en.wikipedia.org/wiki/Social_statistics

28 Ibid.

29 G. Rodr'ıguez, "Linear Models for Continuous Data," Chapter 2, Revised September 2007, http://data.princeton.edu/wws509/notes/c2.pdf.

30 Multilevel Model," Wikipedia, accessed 19 May, 2015, http://en.wikipedia.org/wiki/Multilevel_model.

31 Ibid.

32 "Factor Analysis," Wikipedia, accessed 19 May, 2015, http://en.wikipedia.org/wiki/Factor_analysis

33 "Cluster Analysis," Statistics Textbook, http://documents.software.dell.com/Statistics/Textbook/Cluster-Analysis.

34 *Electronic Statistics Textbook,* (Tulsa, OK: StatSoft, 2013), http://www.statsoft.com/textbook/.

35 Ibid.

36 RAND Corporation, *Predicting Suicide Attacks - Integrating Spatial, Temporal, and Social Features of Terrorist Attack Targets* (Santa Monica, CA: RAND Corporation, 2013)

37 Ibid.

38 Probability theory is the branch of mathematics concerned with probability, and the analysis of random phenomena. In statistics, it is essential to many human activities that involve quantitative analysis of large sets of data.

39 Data mining (an interdisciplinary subfield of Computer Science), is the computational process of discovering patterns in large data sets involving methods at the intersection of artificial intelligence, machine learning, statistics, and database systems. The overall goal of the data mining process is to extract information from a data set and transform it into an understandable structure for further use. Aside from the raw analysis step, it involves database and data management aspects, data pre-processing, model and inference considerations, interestingness metrics, complexity considerations, post-processing of discovered structures, visualization, and online updating. (source: Wikipedia)

40 W. N. Venables, D. M. Smith and the R Core Team, "An Introduction to R," accessed July 1, 2015, http://cran.r-project.org/doc/manuals/R-intro.pdf.

41 Paul Torfs and Claudia Brauer, "A (very) short introduction to R," Wageningen University, The Netherlands, March 3, 2014, accessed July 1, 2015, http://cran.r-project.org/doc/contrib/Torfs+Brauer-Short-R-Intro.pdf.

42 RStudio, https://www.rstudio.com/.

3. The Evolution of Suicide Bombing

The goal of this chapter is to study the development and the advancement of suicide bombing as a global phenomenon and narrow it down in the context of Pakistan, to discover the landscape of terrorist organizations who are active or partially active in suicide attacks. Their locations, motivations, and their affiliations to local and international organizations provide a clear understanding of their funding sources and their global objectives.

3.1. History

Suicide bombing is one of the major growing security concerns of 21st century. The history of suicide bombings by non-state actors goes back to the late 19th century Russia. On 13 March 1881, Ignaty Grinevitsky - a member of the People's Will and the principal assassin of Tsar Alexander II of Russia – watched as his assistant threw a small bomb at the convoy of Tsar Alexander II outside the Winter Palace in St Petersburg. Safely fenced in a carriage made from bullet-proof material as a gift from Napoleon III, the Tsar stepped out, dazed but unhurt. Grinevitsky saw his chance. The young man rushed towards his target, and dropping a bomb at the Tsar's feet, killed both himself and his 62-year-old Emperor. The Tsar's legs were blown off; his stomach ripped open, and his face mutilated and he succumbed to his death in just a few hours.[1] Grinevitsky was the first person in the known history of terrorism who became a truly disreputable suicide bomber.

Suicide bombing has become a favorite terrorist tactic in the war to create fear and distraction between soldiers. In twentieth century, the Japanese military used suicide bombing first time in the Second World War. Unlike suicidal strategies borne of desperation in war, suicide bombing is intentionally employed by terrorists for calculated political effect. After the Second World War, the first major suicide bombing occurred on 23 October 1983 during the Israeli occupation of Lebanon. The truck was packed with 2,000 pounds of explosive and burst into a US Marine base. The truck driver killed himself along with 241 military personnel.[2]

In Palestine - 1993, suicide bombers had been utilized by the two Palestinian groups - Hamas and Palestinian Islamic Jihad - against Israeli targets in an attempt to disrupt talks for a potential peace process. Civilians were the primary target of many of these attacks. 742 civilians were killed, and 4,899 were injured in the course of suicide attacks in Israel and the Palestinian Territories.[3] One group had religious motives and other was motivated by revenge.

It's not necessary that all groups deploy suicide bombing as a national-religious ideology. In Sri Lanka, the Liberation Tigers of Tamil Eelam (LTTE) began using suicide bombings in the late 1980s. LTTE was a secular guerrilla movement. Their objective was the creation of a separate state for Tamil people in Northern and Eastern Sri Lanka.[4]

In 1988, Al Qaeda was formed in Afghanistan[5] with the mission of implementing Sharia law and eliminating the influence of non-Muslim.[6] In 1995, they carried out their first suicide attack in Saudi Arabia targeting a US military base. Al Qaeda leader Osama Bin Laden issued a fatwa in 1998 which declared that all American citizens are the legitimate targets.[7] On August 7th in the same year, they launched twin suicide attacks on the US embassies in Kenya and Tanzania in which 223 people killed. Moreover, in the attacks on the World Trade Center and the Pentagon on September 11, 2001, Al Qaeda used hijacked airliners and, in the aftermath, its battle for global jihad became infamous around the world.

The September, 2011 attacks lead to the complete renovation in US domestic security and foreign policy. The responses to these attacks severely damaged their standing in the Muslim world. Current bombing campaigns against the US and its allies in Afghanistan, Iraq, and Pakistan have some of their roots in the debris of the twin towers.[8]

Iraq is the country worst-hit by suicide bombings over the last decade. At least 1,003 suicide attacks caused civilian casualties in Iraq between 2003 and 2010. Around 12,000 civilians were killed in this time period. The ratio of civilian killed is 60 times more than the soldiers killed. It clearly indicates that civilians are not merely 'collateral damage' but are being deliberately targeted.[9]

The next two graphs as representing the worldwide growth rate of suicide attacks.

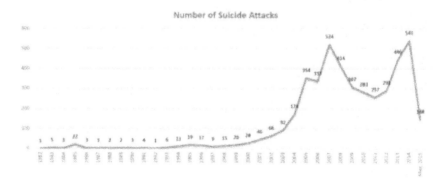

Figure. Suicide Attacks between 1982 – May, 2015

Figure. Suicide Attacks by Country 1982 – May, 2015

3.2. Suicide Bombing in Pakistan

As of May 1ˢᵗ, 2015, Pakistan faced 444 suicide attacks, till May 1, 2015, which killed and injured more than 6,400 and 16,500 individuals respectively. Suicide terrorism started in 1995 in the capital Islamabad and to date has not been able to be eradicated. The first suicide attack in the country was recorded on November 19, 1995 in Islamabad when a suicide attacker struck the Egyptian Embassy with a truck containing explosives. 15 people were killed and around 60 wounded in this massive blast. The bomber was an Egyptian.[10] It's also worth mentioning here that it was the only suicide attack in Pakistan before the War against Terror was started. The second suicide blast was recorded during the regime of former President Musharraf. This attack on November 6, 2000 killed three citizens and injured three others.

The following section will discuss province-wise suicide attacks and some high-profile attacks.

3.2.1. Province-Wise Overview of Suicide Attacks in Pakistan

3.2.1.1. Khyber Pakhtunkha

The KPK province remained the worst affected part of the country with regards to suicide attacks to-date. Since 2002, KPK province had suffered 234 suicide attacks that constitute 48% of the total attacks recorded in the country during the last 12 years. The KPK and FATA combined have faced 68% suicide attacks from 2002 to 2014 collectively. During 2011, KPK witnessed 25 while FATA witnessed nine suicide attacks. Peshawar, which saw 81 suicide attacks, is the most affected city of the KPK. After Peshawar, Bannu is the most affected district of KPK as for as suicide attacks are concerned. During the last 12 years, militants carried out 28 suicide attacks in this district. In 2013 alone, 34 suicide incidents were recorded.

3.2.1.2. Punjab

After KPK, Punjab is also a primary target of suicide bombing in Pakistan. During past nine years, militants carried out 78 suicide attacks in the province, killing 1410, and injuring around 4310. Islamabad, Lahore and Rawalpindi are the main targeted cities of Punjab. In 2009, militants carried out 22 suicide attacks in Punjab, while in 2010 the number of attacks was reduced to 7. Four were recorded in 2011 and three in 2012. In 2013, only a single attack was carried out in Rawalpindi. A significant reduction can be seen in contrast to 2009. One of the main reasons behind this reduction in suicide attacks could be attributed to the security policies adopted by the Punjab government.

The Punjab government holds that within the political arena an electoral culture needs to be fostered that focuses on issues, and not alliances based on bigoted sectarian, tribal and ethnic identities; as a society we must avoid dogmatism and prejudice preached and practiced in the name of religion. As a state, they said, we must develop an effective security policy that is grounded in our indigenous economic and military strength and promotes our strategic interests without relying on jihadists and mercenaries.[11] Though the Punjab government faced severe criticism at the time, it did not affect the strategy of the government. It worked well, and the number of sectarian violence and suicide attacks reduced significantly.

3.2.1.3. Sindh

Militants carried out 30 suicide attacks in Sindh from 2000-2014, all in Karachi – the capital of Sindh. During 2008 to 2010, militants carried out only four suicide attacks in the province but there was an abrupt change in suicide attacks in the year 2011. Karachi faced four attacks in a single year. In May 2011, militants carried out one of the most devastating attacks in the history of Pakistan against Pakistan Navy's Mehran Naval Base. It destroyed two PC Orion Navel aircrafts and killed 13 people, and injured 16 others. The casualties include 11 Navy officials and 1 Ranger.[12] Karachi suffered five attacks in 2013 and six in 2014.

3.2.1.4. Baluchistan

Baluchistan faced the highest number of attacks in the year 2013, when 357 were killed and 760 injured in nineteen attacks. Quetta was the most frequently attacked city of Baluchistan with the ratio of 87.5%. During 2011 militants carried out four suicide attacks in Baluchistan, killing 60 people. Two of these three attacks were aimed at high-value targets such as Deputy Inspector General of Frontier Corp and Deputy Inspector General Police. In one attack of a sectarian nature, the Shia community was targeted outside an Eid Gah on the occasion of Eid-ul-Fitr. Two suicide attacks were recorded in 2008 and 2009 while four were reported in the year 2010 in the province. To date, the province has faced 40 suicide attacks.

3.2.1.5. Federally Administrated Tribal Areas

Till December 2014, Federally Administrated Tribal Areas (FATA) has faced 86 suicide attacks in total. The highest number of suicide causalities was observed in 2010, where 400 people were killed in just thirteen attacks. Seven suicide attacks were recorded in 2011, while attacks gradually increased till 2013. A significant reduction in suicide attacks has been observed in the past year with only three attacks recorded.

3.2.1.6. Azad Kashmir and Gilgit Baltistan

Suicide attacks began in Azad Kashmir in June 2009 continued in the year 2010, but no suicide attack recorded in 2011. The first suicide attack took place in 2009 near Army Public School at Muzaffarabad. The other two suicide attacks occurred in January 2010. These attacks confirm the presence of militants in the region. Till December 2014, they have faced a total of four suicide attacks.

3.2.2. Some High-Profile Attacks in Pakistan

In the history of Pakistan, there are a number of attacks in which the death count was above 50. The primary target of these attacks were the Shia community, Religious/Political Parties, and Frontier Corps. Some varied, high-profile post-2011 attacks are discussed in the following subsections.

3.2.2.1. Deputy Superintendent of Police

The Deputy Superintendent of Police (DSP) of Saddar Circle – Abdul Rashid Khan, was killed in a suicide attack on Kohat Road, Peshawar. One of his gunmen, his driver and two civilians also died in the attack.[13]

3.2.2.2. Army Recruitment Center

On February 10, 2011, it is said that a 15-year-old bomber targeted army personnel during the routine parade at an Army recruitment center in District Mardan in Khyber Pakhtunkhwa, killing 31 and wounding 40 additional soldiers. TTP reclaimed responsibility for the attack.[14]

3.2.2.3. Twin Suicide Bombing Against Frontier Corps

73 paramilitary forces and 17 civilians were killed in twin suicide bombing attacks against frontier corps when they were about to leave from the FC training center at Shabqadar Tehsil in District Charsadda.[15]

3.2.2.4. Attack on Mosque during Friday Prayers: 51 Killed

On August 19, 2011 a suicide attack inside the Mandi khel Masjid in the Jamrud area of Khyber Agency killed 51 individuals and injured105. A young boy of around 15-16 years of age had entered the main hall of the mosque through a window and exploded himself.[16] [17]

3.2.2.5. Suicide Attacks during Eid Prayer

A suicide bombing attack took place in a car on the occasion of Eid-ul-Fitr on August 31, 2011 that killed a minimum of 11 people, and injured 21 in Quetta. The attack took place in the parking lot of a mosque when hundreds of Muslims were leaving after the Eid-ul-Fitr prayer. The attacker wanted to hit the explosive-laden car into Eid Gah (the mosque), but the explosion occurred in the parking lot, due to "tight security" around the mosque.[18]

3.2.2.6. Attack on DIG Frontier Corps

Two suicide attacks occurred outside the official residence of the DIG Frontier Corps (FC) on September 8, 2011. The attacks took the lives of at least 28 people, including an FC Colonel and the wife of the Deputy Inspector General of FC. The DIG, Brigadier Farrukh Shahzad, and 16 FC personnel were among 82 people injured in the attacks. The attacks took place in a high-security area where several government offices and residences of senior officials, including the Governor's House, Chief Minister's House, residences of IG Police and chief secretary are located.[19]

3.2.2.7. Suicide Attack on Funeral prayer On September 15, 2011

On September 15, 2011 a suicide attack during the funeral prayer of tribal elder Bakht Khan, in Jandol area of Lower Dir district of Khyber Pakhtunkhwa province killed 35 individuals, and injured 71 civilians.[20]

3.2.2.8. Suicide Attack on Mosque

March 24, 2012, a suicide bomber blew himself at a mosque in Kolay village of Tirah Valley, Khyber Agency. At least 13 were killed and 7 others wounded. The mosque, run by Lashkar-e-Islam (LeI) and Tehreek-e-Taliban Pakistan (TTP) claimed the responsibility of the attack.[21][22] Lashkar-e-Islam and Ansarul Islam and the TTP extremist groups are known to compete for influence in Tirah Valley.

3.2.2.9. Quetta Explosions

Two explosions that occurred on January 10, 2013, killed at least 81, and injured 121 in blasts. The first attack took places in a snooker club and the second took place after 10 minutes outside the snooker club when rescue workers, people and police started taking the injured to the hospital. The majority of causalities happened in the second blast. Lashkar-e-Jhangvi claimed its responsibility. Five police personnel, including a senior police officer, and three media men also lost their lives in the second blast. The majority of the people killed belonged to the Hazara Shia community.[23]

3.2.2.10. Church Attack in Peshawar

On September 22, 2014, twin suicide attacks killed at least 78, and injured over a 100 people at All Saints Church in Peshawar. Most of the injured were in critical condition. Blasts occurred when the religious service had just ended. There are about 200,000 Christians in the province and 70,000 of them live in Peshawar.[24]

3.2.2.11. Militant Siege of Peshawar School

On December 16, 2014, militants attacked an army school in Peshawar. At least 141 people were killed, most of them children of grades 1 – 10. DG Inter-Services Public Relations (ISPR) Major General Asim Bajwa said, "They have hit at the heart of the nation, but let me reiterate they can't in any way diminish the will of this great nation."[25] Later, TTP claimed responsibility for this attack.

3.3. Terrorist Groups in Pakistan

In Pakistan, suicide bombings originated in 1994. They gradually increased with time as and when terrorist groups formulated. It is important to know how terrorist groups are formed in Pakistan. This section studies the evolution of suicide terrorist organizations based in Pakistan, focusing on how and when they were formed, and with what motivations.

3.3.1. Al-Qaeda

Al Qaeda (AQ) was initially comprised of Afghan mujahedeen fighting against Soviet influence in Afghanistan from the late 1970s through the 1980s. It was founded by Osama bin Laden on August 1988. It is one of the longest-operating jihadist militant organizations in the Middle East and Asia, with followers and support around the world. AQ has carried out a number of attacks around the world, most notably the hijackings and bombings of the USS Cole (2000), World Trade Center in New York City (2001), Istanbul bombings (2003), and the London Train bombings (2005).[26]

The motives of AQ are to get rid of Western influence from the Muslim world, and pursues the setting up of an Islamic caliphate that imposes strict Sunni interpretation of Shariah law. AQ is organized in more than 100 different countries. They primarily target political figures who oppose AQ operations, and foreign forces and civilians who are seen as a threat to the Muslim world or to the establishment of Shariah-based Islamic rules in the Muslim countries. The September 11, 2011 attacks have left a legacy of long-term effects and have wreaked damages of over $1 trillion in New York City alone.[27]

AQ has strong ties with terrorist groups in Pakistan i.e. Jaish-e-Mohammad (JeM), Lashkar-e-Taiba (LeT), Harkat-ul-Jihad al-Islami (HuJI), Tehreek-e-Taliban Pakistan (TTP), the Taliban.

3.3.2. Lashkar-e-Islam

Lashkar-e-Islam (LeI) is an active militant group in Khyber Agency of Pakistan's Federally Administered Tribal Areas. It began as an anti-Barelvi sectarian group in 2004, led by Haji Namdar and Mufti Shakir by having Deoband Ideology.[28] LeI was engaged in clashed with a Barelvi group in agency, led by Pir Saif-ur-Rehman. When the clashed increased, a series of Jirgas (elders meeting) were held to sort out the issue and forced both leaders to leave Bara. Two groups of the agency, Lashkar-e-Islam and Ansar-ul-Islam began to fight with each other, as leaders left.

In 2008, LeI become a rival of Tehreek-e-Taliban Pakistan (TTP) when Haji Namdar was killed by TTP. Strategically Khyber Agency has its importance for both the government and the Taliban as the main land route to Afghanistan and the Central Asia states via the Khyber Pass. It's the only supply route to U.S. and NATO troops in Afghanistan.[29] Because of strategic importance of Khyber Agency, many times TTP leaders tried to align their movements with LeI, but they refused each time. The contention between LeI and TTP still continued and this make LeI an anti-Taliban group. LeI was involved in the terrorist attack at shrine of the famous Pukhtun poet Rehman Baba in Hazarkhwani, near Peshawar on March 5, 2009.

3.3.3. Ansar-ul-Islam

Ansar-ul-Islam (AI) is a Barelvi Sunni Muslim group in the Khyber Agency, Federally Administered Tribal Areas. It was founded in 2004 by Pir Saif-ur-Rehman – an Afghan Sufi, and set up his headquarter in the remote Tirrah valley of the agency. They are rivals of LeI. Both groups face many contentious situation in the region. AI was banned in June, 2008 by the government of Pakistan.[30]

Latif Afridi, a secular politician from the region, says that Ansar ul-Islam is fighting against a coalition of the Al-Qaeda, TTP and Lashkar-e-Islam. He said, "They are not terrorists. They have never been involved in terrorist activities such as suicide bombings. They are just fighting for protecting their region. They have always helped the government in its efforts to establish peace in the region."[31]

3.3.4.   Harkat-ul-Jihad al-Islami

The Harkat-ul-Jihad al-Islami (HuJI) is a Pakistan-based Deobandi militant group with the central aim of liberating Jammu and Kashmir from India and making them part of Pakistan. While the exact formation date of the group is not known, it has origins in the Soviet-Afghan war around 1980 and is currently led by Qari Saifullah Akhtar. HuJI has extensive ties to both the Taliban and al-Qaeda, as well as to numerous other organizations.[32]

HuJI has operated many small and large-scale suicide bombings and assassinations, particularly in the Indo-Pak region and has an active affiliate in Bangladesh. HuJI handled the suicide bombing of the U.S. Consulate in Karachi on March 2, 2006, killing four people including U.S. diplomat David Foy.[33]

3.3.5.   Sipah-e-Sahaba Pakistan

In September 1985, when the Shia-Sunni conflict was escalating in the city of Punjab – Jhang, Sipah-e-Sahaba Pakistan (SSP) came into being. Right after gaining support from the regime of Zia-ul-Haq and received funding from Saudia Arabia, SSP became the most prominent anti-Shia militant group of Pakistan. Since then, it is being involved in terrorism, violent sectarianism and local and national electoral politics.[34]

The SSP has connections with many other terrorist groups, including Jaish-e-Mohammad (JeM), Lashkar-e-Taiba (LeT), Harkatul Mujahideen, and al Qaeda. Since September 2011, the SSP and LeJ have become "a mainstay of al Qaeda planning in Pakistan." [35]

On February 4, 2008, Militants bombed a bus carrying security personnel near the General Headquarters of the Pakistani Army in Rawalpindi. SSP claimed its responsibility. [36]

3.3.6.   Jaish-e-Mohammad

Jaish-e-Mohammad (JeM) is a Pakistan-based Islamic extremist group founded by Maulana Masood Azhar in January 2000. JeM uses violence to pursue its stated objectives of uniting Kashmir with Pakistan and the "destruction" of India and America. Since its inception, JeM's terrorist activities have rapidly gained momentum in the Indian state of Jammu and Kashmir. Indian intelligence officials hold JeM responsible for various terrorist strikes against India. In 2003, the U.S. designated JeM, a foreign terrorist organization, and Pakistani authorities subsequently banned it. JeM allegedly continues to operate as of 2011.[37]

JeM has strong links with the Sipah-e-Sahaba Pakistan (SSP) and also has ideological and strategic ties with Lashkar-e-Jhangvi (LeJ).[38] JeM became a rival of Harkat-ul-Mujahideen (HuM) after the split from HuM to form JeM in 2000 in light of internal divisions between Punjabis and other ethnic groups. The HuM and JeM continued to coexist despite the fact that several top members from HuM left the organization to join JeM. JeM is a rival of Hizb-ul-Mujahideen (HM) for influence in Kashmir and also rivals with Lashkar-e-Taiba (LeT).[39]

JeM majorly operates in disputed areas of Kashmir. But on December 25, 2003, they attempted the assassination of Pakistani President Musharraf by a car bomb in Pakistan. 18 persons were killed, and 40 injured during a second assassination attempt on President Pervez Musharraf.[40] Another attack in January 2014, on a passenger bus carrying Shia Pilgrims from Taftan, a town in Baloshictan bordering with Iran, responsibility claimed by JeM.[41]

3.3.7.   Lashkar-e-Jhangvi

Lashkar-e-Jhangvi (LeJ) is an anti-Shiite terrorist group in Pakistan that maintains strong ties with al-Qaeda. LeJ was founded by former

Sipah-e-Sahaba Pakistan (SSP) officials Riaz Basra, Akram Lahori, and Malik Ishaque. It was formally split in the mid-1990s, to protest an emerging dialog between the SSP and Shiite parties. LeJ has carried out many suicide attacks on minority groups in Pakistan with the aim of establishing Pakistan as an orthodox Deobandi state. In 2001, Pakistan officially banned LeJ. But it continues to play a central role in the escalating cycle of sectarian violence in Pakistan. Now it is said that LeJ has allied with the Tehrik-e-Taliban Pakistan (TTP).[42]

In September 2008, a truck bomb exploded near the Marriott Hotel in Islamabad, and LeJ claimed responsibility for it.[43]

3.3.8. Tehreek-e-Taliban Pakistan

Tehreek-e-Taliban Pakistan (TTP) is the Pakistan-based Taliban organization that operates out of Pakistan's provinces and carries out attacks only within Pakistan. It is the largest militant group in Pakistan. The organization was established on December 13, 2007, following a meeting of tribal elders and 40 senior militants from all over Pakistan.[44] In the perspective of the formulation of TTP, we cannot neglect the incident of Lal Masjid in July 2007 that had occurred in the same year. It can be inferred that the formation of TTP is the outcome of Lal Masjid incident and reflects the majority of those sympathetic to Lal Masjid.

The main goal of TTP's establishment was to unite the various groups of the Pakistan Taliban in order to shape synchronized attacks on NATO/ISAF forces in Afghanistan. Baitullah Mehsud was appointed as the leader of TTP.[45]

TTP has strong associations to al-Qaeda and heavily relies on it for financial, logistical and ideological support. TTP apparently trains militants, and finances al-Qaeda operations, and aids in the carrying out of attacks in both Afghanistan and Pakistan. TTP had been accused by the government of Pakistan in the involvement of the murder of Former Pakistani Prime Minister Benazir Bhutto, but TTP has denied any involvement.[46]

Notes

1   Henry Dodd, "A short history of suicide bombing," *Action on Armed Violence*, Aug 23, 2013, accessed May 9, 2015, https://aoav.org.uk/2013/a-short-history-of-suicide-bombings/.

2   Henry Dodd, "A short history of suicide bombing," *Action on Armed Violence*, Aug 23, 2013, accessed May 9, 2015, https://aoav.org.uk/2013/a-short-history-of-suicide-bombings/.

3   Ibid.

4   Ibid.

5   "Al-Qaeda." International Encyclopedia of the Social Sciences. 2008. Encyclopedia.com. (June 9, 2015). http://www.encyclopedia.com/doc/1G2-3045300065.html

6   Henry Dodd, "A short history of suicide bombing," *Action on Armed Violence*, Aug 23, 2013, accessed May 9, 2015, https://aoav.org.uk/2013/a-short-history-of-suicide-bombings/.

7   Ibid.

8   James Kiras, "Suicide Bombing," Encyclopedia Britannica, Aug 07, 2014, accessed May 9, 2015, http://www.britannica.com/EBchecked/topic/736115/suicide-bombing.

9   Ibid.

10   Abdulhadi Hairan, "The History of Suicide Attacks in Pakistan," Ground Report, 2007, accessed May 10, 2015, http://groundreport.com/the-history-of-suicide-attacks-in-pakistan/.

11   Sarah Khan, "Some legal aspects of PML-N's alliance with Sipah-e-Sahaba," *Let Us Build Pakistan*, March 13, 2010, accessed on Aug 25, 2014, http://lubpak.com/archives/7077.

12   "Terrorists attack on PNS Mehran: Malik," *The News*, May 22, 2011, accessed on Aug 25, 2014, http://www.thenews.com.pk/NewsDetail.aspx?ID=15943

13   "Suicide attack kills DSP Rashid Khan," *The News*, January 31, 2011, accessed on Aug 25, 2014, http://www.thenews.com.pk

14 Bill Roggio, "Teenage suicide bomber kills 28 army personnel," *The Long War Journal*, February 10, 2011, accessed on Aug 25, 2014, http://www.longwarjournal.org/archives/2011/02/taliban_suicide_bomb_18.php

15 "Twin blasts kill more than 80 in Charsadda," *Dawn*, May 14, 2011, accessed on Aug 25, 2014, http://www.dawn.com

16 "Suicide Blast in Mosque during Friday prayer," *Dawn*, August 20, 2011, accessed on Aug 25, 2014, http://www.dawn.com

17 "Khyber agency blast in Jamrud Mosque," *Pakistan Tribune*, August 19, 2011, accessed on Aug 25, 2014, http://tribune.com.pk

18 "Suicide strike on Lower Dir funeral," *Dawn*, August 31, 2011, accessed Aug 12, 2014, http://www.dawn.com

19 "Suicide attack kills DSP Rashid Khan," *Dawn*, accessed on Aug 25, 2014, http://www.dawn.com

20 "Suicide strike on Lower Dir funeral," *Dawn*, September 16, 2011, accessed Aug 12, 2014, http://www.dawn.com

21 "Suicide attack on Mosque," *Sach TV*, March 24, 2012, accessed June 13, 2015, http://www.saach.tv/2012/03/24/suicide-bomber-attacked-mosque/.

22 Taliban bomber kills 13 'extremists' in Khyber region," *The Express Tribune*, March 24, 2012, accessed June 13, 2015, http://tribune.com.pk/story/354349/taliban-bomber-kills-13-extremists-in-khyber-region/.

23 "At least 93 lives lost in Quetta explosions," *Dawn*, January 11, 2013, accessed June 13, 2015, http://www.dawn.com/news/777830/at-least-93-lives-lost-in-quetta-explosions.

24 "78 killed, over 100 injured in Peshawar Church Attack," *The Express Tribune*, accessed June 13, 2015, http://tribune.com.pk/story/607734/fifteen-dead-in-suicide-attack-outside-peshawar-church/.

25 Militant siege of Peshawar School ends, 141 killed, Dawn, accessed June 13, 2015, http://www.dawn.com/news/1151203.

26 "Al Qaeda," Mapping Militant Organizations, accessed June 12, 2015, http://web.stanford.edu/group/mappingmilitants/cgi-bin/groups/view/21.

27 Ibid.

28 "Lashkar-e-Islam," Mapping Militant Organizations, accessed June 12, 2015, http://web.stanford.edu/group/mappingmilitants/cgi-bin/groups/view/445.

29 Ibid.

30 Ansar ul-Islam, Wikipedia, accessed June 13, 2015, https://en.wikipedia.org/wiki/Ansar_ul-Islam.

31 Pakistan's Islamist Militia Ansar Ul-Islam and Its Fight for Influence, *Radio Free Europs Radio Liberty*, January 2013, accessed June 13, 2015, http://www.rferl.org/content/pakistan-ansar-ul-islam-taliban-ttp/24886662.html.

32 "Harkat-ul-Jihad al-Islami," Mapping Militant Organizations, accessed May 22, 2015, http://web.stanford.edu/group/mappingmilitants/cgi-bin/groups/view/217.

33 Ibid.

34 "Sipah-e-Sahaba Pakistan," Mapping Militant Organizations, accessed May 22, 2015, http://web.stanford.edu/group/mappingmilitants/cgi-bin/groups/view/147.

35 Ibid.

36 Ibid.

37 "Jaish-e-Mohammad," Mapping Militant Organizations, accessed May 22, 2015, http://web.stanford.edu/group/mappingmilitants/cgi-bin/groups/view/95.

38 Ibid.

39 Ibid.

40 "Pakistan Timeline – Year 2003," SATP, accessed May 23, 2015, http://www.satp.org/satporgtp/countries/pakistan/timeline/2003.htm.

41 "Quetta: 2 dead as sucide bomber targets pilgrims returning from Iran", *The Express Tribune*, January 1, 2014, accessed June 13, 2015, http://tribune.com.pk/story/653388/powerful-blast-heard-in-quetta/.

42 "Lashkar-e-Jhangvi," Mapping Militant Organizations, accessed May 22, 2015, http://web.stanford.edu/group/mappingmilitants/cgi-bin/groups/view/215.

43 Ibid.

44 "Tehreek-i-Taliban Pakistan," Mapping Militant Organizations, accessed May 22, 2015, http://web.stanford.edu/group/mappingmilitants/cgi-bin/groups/view/105.

45 Ibid.

46 Ibid.

4. Data Collection of Suicide Bombing

In general, data is defined as a collection of facts, information, and statistics that can be used for references and analysis to draw a conclusion.

Data collection is a crucial and systematic approach to gathering information from a variety of sources in order to get a complete and accurate picture of an area of interest. It enables the researcher to answer the stated questions, test hypotheses and evaluate outcomes. The methods of data collection can vary by the field of study, but accurate data collection is essential to maintain the integrity of research. However, the goal of data collection is to capture quality evidence that then translates to rich data analysis and allows the building of a convincing and credible answer to questions that have been posed.

In the collection of suicide bombing data, Qualitative and Quantitative methods were used to generate new and objective data that will help to perform detailed analysis on the events of the attacks. Before moving on to the data collection phase, it is important to study the existing work on suicide bombing datasets.

4.1. International Organizations

It has been observed that it is international organizations that are primarily keeping the count of suicide attacks. Here we will analyze the international organizations and the variables they maintain in the context of suicide terrorism.

4.1.1. Chicago Project on Security and Terrorism (CPOST)

The University of Chicago, under the Chicago Project on Security and Terrorism[1] (CPOST) initiative, maintains a searchable database, for all suicide attacks (1982 – Jan 2015). Being one of the most comprehensive and publicly available dataset, CPOST has information on factors such as the following.

Variables	Description
Date	The incident date
Location of Attack	Where the incident occurs
Target Type	Who is the primary target
Weapon Type	Which weapon used
Group	Attack claimed by
Campaign	Attack happens during which campaign

Table. CPOST Variables

CPOST also maintains a map that depicts all the suicide attacks that occurred during 1982 to 2013. The map helps pinpoint the geographic location of the attack, and the key provides an overview of the number of casualties in a particular attack.

4.1.2. International Terrorism: Attributes of Terrorist Events

The International Terrorism: Attributes of Terrorist Events (ITERATE) project quantifies data on the characteristics of transnational terrorist groups, their activities that carry international impact and the environment in which they operate.[2] This data is available only for the Duke Community via ITERATE license agreement.

4.1.3. Global Terrorism Database Portal

Global Terrorism Database (GTD) Portal is an open-source database that includes information on terrorist events around the world. They have kept data since 1970 and have maintained 137 variables against more than 125,000 cases. GTD portal is the project of National Consortium for the Study of Terrorism And Responses to Terrorism (START).[3]

As the GTD portal covers all kind of the terrorist attacks and scenarios from the globe, the number of variables is maintained accordingly. For Pakistan, they recorded the attacks till Nov 2011. The following primary variables have been maintained in the GTD portal, and these variables have been further sub divided.[4]

Variables	Description
ID & Date	The incident ID and date
Incident Information	Incident information
Incident Location	Comprehensive details provide for location
Attack Information	Comprehensive details provide for attack information
Weapon Information	Comprehensive details provide for weapon information
Targets and Perpetrators	Comprehensive details provide for targets and perpetrators
Casualties & Consequences	Comprehensive details provide for causalities and consequences
Additional Information & Sources	Additional information and sources about the incident provided

Table. GTD Variables

4.1.4.   RAND Corporation - Natural Security and Research Division

The RAND Cooperation is a nonprofit, nonpartisan organization, committed to the public interest. The RAND National Security Research Division (NSRD) conducts research and analysis for all national security sponsors other than the U.S. Air Force and the Army.[5] It looks at different aspects of threats and terrorism all over the world. Their project RAND Database of Worldwide Terrorism Incidents (RDWTI) is a compilation of data from 1968 through 2009. It is free and publically accessible for research and analysis. The variables, they maintained is presented in next table.

Variables	Description
Date	The incident date
Country	Where the incident occurs
City	Name of the city
Weapon Type	Weapon used for attack
Perpetrator	Who is the perpetrator
Fatalities	No. of people killed in attacks
Injuries	No. of people injured in attacks
Description	Details of the attack

Table. RAND NSRD Variables

4.1.5.   South Asia Terrorism Portal

The South Asia Terrorism Portal (SATP) was launched in March 2000. It is the largest, most comprehensive, searchable and regularly updated database on all available information related to terrorism, low-intensity warfare and ethnic/communal/sectarian strife in South Asia.[6]

This project is the initiative of the Institute for Conflict Management (ICM). ICM provides consultancy services on terrorism and internal security to the Indian government and abroad. It was established in 1997 in New Delhi, India and registered as a non-profit, non-governmental organization supported by voluntary contributions and project aid.[7]

SATP doesn't provide us with variables on Suicide Bombing data for useful for an appropriate analysis. They provide the following variables.

Variables	Description
Date	The incident date
Place	Where the incident occurs
Incidents	The headline news is provided in this field
Killed	No. of people killed
Injured	No. of injured people

Table. SATP Variables

4.2. National Organizations

Among national organizations, we found a single body that maintains data on suicide bombing.

4.2.1. Pak Institute of Peace Studies

The Pak Institute of Peace Studies[8] (PIPS) is an independent, non-profit and non-government think-tank. PIPS conducts wide-ranging research and analysis on the conflicts of a political, social and religious nature. They have also maintained the data regarding suicide bombing, but on a very low scale. Following are the variables they maintain.

Variables	Description
Date	The incident date
Place	Where the incident occurs
Target	The headline news is provided in this field
Killed	No. of people killed
Injured	No. of injured people
Suspected/Responsible Groups	Details of the suspected groups

Table. PIPS Variables

The main drawback with PIPS is that they do not following data entry standards. Rather, they merely document incidents. PIPS Data Format represents an example of the inappropriate format of data. Note that the 'Suspected/Responsible Groups' variable is abstruse because 'Suspected and Responsible Group' has to be two different variables. Moreover, this is not comprehensive data that would be of help to researchers in analysis.

4.3. Concerns

Pakistan lacks a comprehensive national database for terrorism or suicide bombing, and needs to rely on the figures given by international bodies. It is the need of the time to validate the data of victims with the international media and judge the accuracy of the international media. Pakistan needs to keep count of its casualties and maintain proper records of destruction caused by attacks. Suicide bombing, after all, is our dispute and it is imperative that we look into it from all aspects.

4.4.　Method used for Data Collection

Information about all related incidents such as suicide bombings, planted bombs, drone attacks, and other possible disturbances including firings and killings is publically available. All the information has been collected from printed media, electronic media, and the internet. The sources of data include local and international news channels and papers such as Daily Dawn, Daily Jang, and Daily Express News from Pakistan. Additionally, it also includes non-Pakistani news organizations such as CNN, BBC, and Al-Jazeera.

Figure below has presented the practice we used to identified feature-set and record them.

All the information regarding suicide terrorist events is gathered using a variety of means, such as by saving clippings or internet data. We have included only those attacks that can be verified by at least two of the sources mentioned above.

4.5.　Pakistan Body Count

The website of the Pakistan Body Count (PBC)[9] provides a complete history and timeline of suicide bombing and drone attacks in Pakistan. Data is collected from media reports, and the internet. All data is publicly available and includes no classified data. This is an effort to show the world the intensity of suicide bombing and drone attacks in Pakistan.

With the collaboration of the PBC organization, the researcher has been working on the latest version of suicide bombing data and keeping it up-to-date. The variables that have been maintained so far are shown in the following table.

Category				Variable	Description
				Sr. No.	Attacks counter
				Date of Attack	Incident date
Killed				Min.	Min record deaths
				Max.	Max recorded deaths
Injured				Min.	Min recorded injuries
				Max.	Max recorded injuries
Location				Place	Type of place
				City/Agency	City
				Province	Province
				Address	Address
				Geolocation	Longitude and latitude of the location
				Time of Attack	Time of the incident
	Bomber(s)			No. of Bomber(s)	No of bombers at the incident place
				Suspected Age	Suspected age of the bomber
				Other Weapon(s)	Was the bomber holding any other weapon
				Origin/Identity	Bombers identity
				Type	How the bomb got exploded (e.g. by foot, by vehicle etc.)
	About Bomb			Weight – KG	Bomb weight
				No.	No of bombs exploded
				No. of Foreigner	No. of foreigner being killed
Target Type				Primary Target	Who was the primary target
				Sectarian	Whether the attack type is sectarian
				Religious	Whether the attack type is religious
Claim				Who	Which terrorist organization claim for the attack
				Statement	What statement was given
				Speaker	Who was to spoken person
				Occasion	On which occasion, incident happened
				Hospital-Victims taken to	The name of the hospital where victims were taken to
				Notes	Some additional notes about incident

Table. PBC Collected Variables

4.6. Leads of PBC Suicide Bombing Data

The PBC has certain advantages over the GTD and SATP data.

- Maintains the precise time entry
- Contains detailed location information
- Maintain the profile of bomber
- Provides details about the bomb
- Identifies whether the attack was sectarian
- Provides details of the occasion

4.7. Variables to Extend

We can also incorporate the following variables to expand the database and to carry out extensive analysis, as these will cover a more comprehensive picture of the suicide attack.

4.7.1. Explosion Type

The suicide bombings have been grouped into three basic categories of devices:[10]

- a. Bomber Actuated Improvised Explosive Device (IED)s Carried in Bag, Box or Other Object
- b. Bomber Actuated IED Worn Under or as Part of Clothing of Bomber
- c. Bomber Actuated IED Concealed in Vehicle

The frequency of victims is highly dependent on the explosive type because when the attack happens, the explosive material become shrapnel and causes more destruction. How an explosive material works is presented below, by illustrating the example of a pressure cooker.

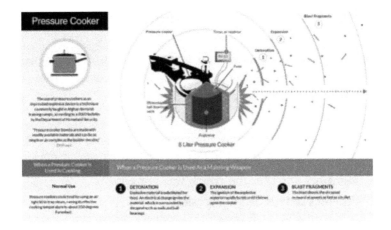

Figure. Example of a Pressure Cooker for Explosion

4.7.2.   Quantity of Trinitrotoluene (TNT)

The forensic department can identify how much TNT was used in the explosion bomb. It directly influences the efficiency of blast expansion.

4.7.3.   Injuries Type

This variable is very crucial for the in-depth analysis of the attack. Each suicide attack causes different types of injuries. It highly depends on the kind of explosion and quantity of TNT that was used in the attack. Figure below represents a summary of the types of injuries that occur.

Figure. Blast Injuries to the Human Body

4.7.4. Type of Shrapnel

In suicide attacks, more than 90% of the victims injured are hit by the bomb shrapnel. The most widely used and the most dangerous shrapnel consists of steel ball bearings 3-7 millimeters in diameter. Apart from steel balls, nails, screws, nuts and washers are also used.[11]

4.7.5. Perpetrator

Each terrorist group is also associated with specific patterns. With the inspection of TNT quantity and injury types, the perpetrator can be identified.

4.7.6. Ethnicity Type

It would cover the ethnicity of the people that are being targeted. For instance if a Punjabi was targeted in Karachi, it is considered similar to a Punjabi attacked in Peshawar; the Ethnic Type under attack was Punjabi.

4.7.7. Motives

It is presumed that there are always some motives that propel the suicide attacks to action. For instance, it can be "The attack was motivated against the Lal Masjid Operation."

4.7.8. Property Damage/ Overall Damage

It would include the damage in monetary terms. For instance if the damage was bigger than $1M, it would be categorized appropriately.

These variables were very time consuming to be maintained in the current database of suicide bombing. However, their recording and maintenance is worth mentioning. This data will broaden our analysis in the long run. For example, the analysis of Explosion Type, Quantity of TNT and Types of Injury can prove useful in identifying the common attacks pattern that can gradually contribute to identifying the terrorist groups.

4.8. Limitations

The most significant barrier to maintaining all these variables is the need to visit each hospital from where the medical records of blast injured victims can be obtained. In addition, the police or forensics labs of the affected areas need to be contacted or visited to collect this data. Often, police and hospitals are averse to allowing researchers access to such data because of security reasons. They are not authorized to outsource to anyone until an influential reference is used.

In order to ascertain motives, an extensive news reader is required to relate the events (implement the causation approach) with the attacks. And for the Property Damage/Overall Damage variable, one needs to visit the place and enquire the property rate by approaching the property dealer of that area, as Pakistan lacks an organized or central platform for real estate valuation.

4.9. Dataset of Suicide Bombing

The dataset of the suicide bombing has been maintained in Comma Separated Values (CSV) file format. Data from CSV file format can easily be imported into various computer applications. See the Appendix A for a complete database of suicide bombing.

Notes

1   "Chicago Project on Security and Terrorism (CPOST)," Suicide Attack Database, UChicago CPOST, accessed March 25, 2015, http://cpostdata.uchicago.edu/search_new.php.

2   "International Terrorism: Attributes of Terrorist Events (ITERATE)," Duke University Library, accessed 24 March, 2015, http://library.duke.edu/data/collections/iterate.

3   "Global Terrorism Database", START, accessed March 20, 2015, http://www.start.umd.edu/gtd/

4   "Codebook: Inclusion Criteria and Variables," GTD, START, accessed 25 March, http://www.start.umd.edu/gtd/downloads/Codebook.pdf.

5   "RAND database of Worldwide Terrorism Incidents (RDWTI)," RAND Corporation, accessed March 24, 2015, http://www.rand.org/nsrd/projects/terrorism-incidents.html.

6   "South Asia Terrorism Portal," accessed March 21, 2013, http://www.satp.org/satporgtp/satp/index.html

7   "Institute for Conflict Management," accessed on March 22, 2015, http://www.satp.org/satporgtp/icm/index.html.

8   Pak Institute of Peace Studies, "Pak Institute of Peace Studies, Independent Think-Tank in Pakistan," accessed on April 3, 2015, http://san-pips.com/.

9   Pakistan Body Count, http://pakistanbodycount.org/.

10 FBI, Bomb Data Center, "Improvised Explosive Devices Used in Suicide Bombing Incidents," Public Intelligence, accessed March 23, 2015, https://info.publicintelligence.net/bombcenteried.pdf.

11 "Preparation of a Suicide Bomber," The Mechanics of a Living Bombs, War Online, accessed March 23, 2015, http://www.waronline.org/en/terror/suicide.htm

5. Data Analysis of Suicide Bombing

Terrorism has already taken its toll across the world. A colossal amount of causalities and deaths have been the prime focus of terrorist groups. The eruption of terrorism has been hovering over Pakistan for years now. Long term consequences of frequent suicide attacks in Pakistan have already incapacitated the nation. The society has been desensitized in such a way that what appeared violent to Pakistanis in past does not seem violent anymore. It happens when the people are constantly living under fear, and when the security of masses becomes an unreality. The realities of dehumanization lead to retaliation and there comes a time when retaliation begins to take shape inside our brains, the kind which pushes us to break the barrier of humanity. Thus, the nation is slowly destroyed.

The goal of this chapter is to identify the useful insights and hidden patterns from data on suicide bombing.

5.1. Preprocessing - Data Cleaning

Data understanding and data cleaning is an essential phase that needs to be accomplished before heading to data analysis. For data cleaning, data understanding is essential. Data needs to be in the proper format, so the data analysis can be performed effectively. Almost 70% of time is spent in just the data cleaning task. In cleaning, we usually perform the following tasks:

- Remove Not Available (NA) values
- Remove disparities in data
- Leveling the factors
- Predicting the missing values
- Fix the data types
- Fix the format
- The addition of further variables may be required for analysis

The number of people killed in the last 12 years as a result of suicide bombing stands at approximately 7,227, with 15,326 wounded. Given the fatalities figure, on average, at least 1 person was killed, and 4 people were injured every day in suicide bombing, from last 10 years. 76% of those killed were only from KPK.

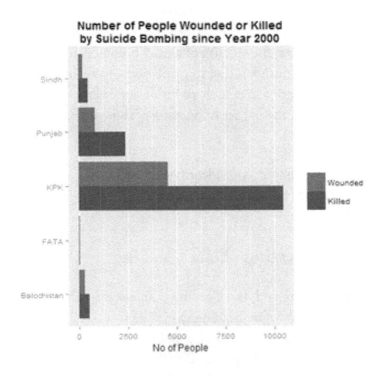

Figure. Suicide Bombing since 2000

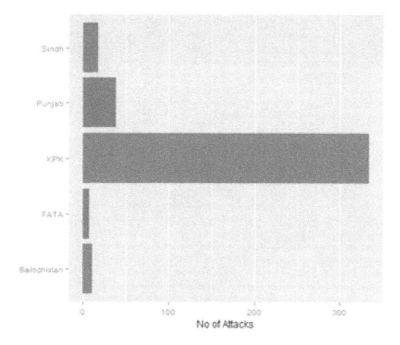

Figure. No. of Attacks

It is clearly evident from the plot above that the largest number of attacks happened in KPK. Punjab comes second. 47% of the attacks happened in KPK, which means that, on average, there has been an attack every week in the last 10 years.

The frequency of deaths in each province has been presented in "Provinces-wise Death Rate". KPK has been unfortunate to have highest number of people killed. The maximum number of deaths occurred in the range of 10 – 18, with approximately 200 suicide attack incidents.

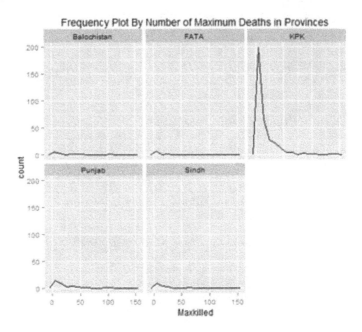

Figure. Provinces-wise Death Rate

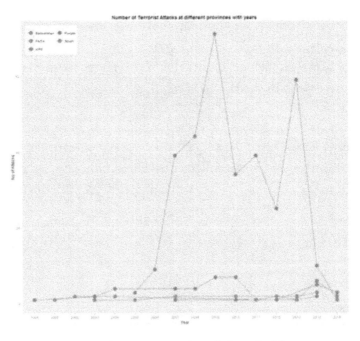

Figure. Province-wise Attach Rate by Year

Province-wise Attach Rate by Year depicts, KPK has been worse off in all years, followed by Punjab. The trend that emerges is that the attacks increased in the year 2007, the same year when Tehreek Taliban Pakistan (TTP) came into being. These can be inferred to be in retaliation to the attack on Lal Masjid Attack, which co-incidentally happened in the same year. The responsibility for the Lal Masjid operation was claimed by no organization and on July 6, 2008 a revenge suicide attack occurred on the first anniversary of the siege of Lal Masjid, killing 18 policemen and a civilian in total and leaving over 40 people injured.

The analysis further digs down to the year-wise comparison of suicide attacks in provinces. This has been represented in figure below.

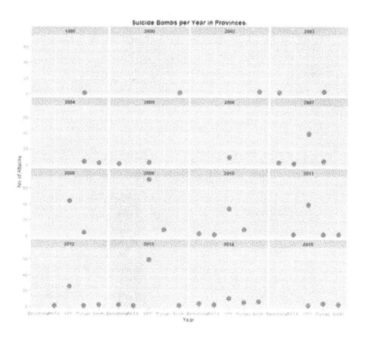

Figure. Yearly Attacks Province-wise

In figure "Box-plot City-wise Suicide Attacks", the box plot shows that the city of Peshawar was attacked by the highest number of suicide bombers. Quetta follows at second place. The box plot displays the distribution of data based on the five statistical summary: minimum, first quartile, median, third quartile, and maximum. The detailed chart has been represented titled "City-wise Suicide Attacks" and the list of the top 10 attacked cities, along with the number of attacks is represented in table.

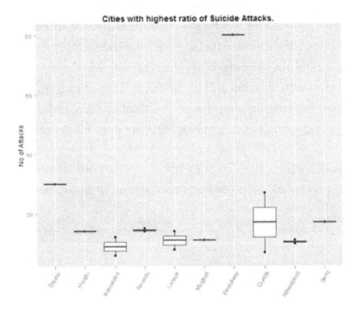

Figure. Box-plot City-wise Suicide Attacks

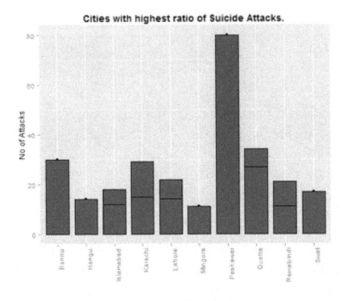

Figure. City-wise Suicide Attacks

Province	City	Total Number of Attacks
KPK	Peshawar	80
Baluchistan	Quetta	34
KPK	Bannu	30
Sindh	Karachi	29
Punjab	Lahore	22
Punjab	Rawalpindi	21
Punjab	Islamabad	18
KPK	Swat	17
KPK	Hangu	14
KPK	Mingora	11

Table. Top 10 Attacked Cities

In the scatter plot of people killed by Suicide attacks in particular months and years, it appears that year 2007, 2008 and 2009 were the deadliest. As Peshawar and Quetta have faced highest number of attacks, the one reason could be to provide the corridor of NATO supply.

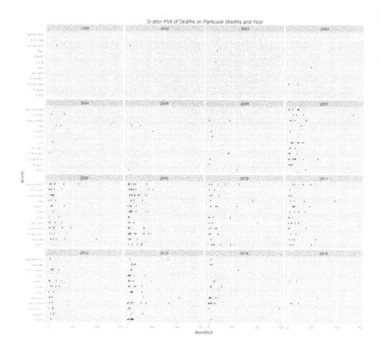

Figure. Death Rate Month and Year-wise

5.2. The most likely weekday, province-wise

"Death Rate Month and Year-wise" shows the frequency of attacks by weekday for each of the provinces. The total height represents the total number of attacks on a particular weekday and the relative height of the colored portion shows the relative contribution of a particular province. All provinces show very similar trends by weekdays.

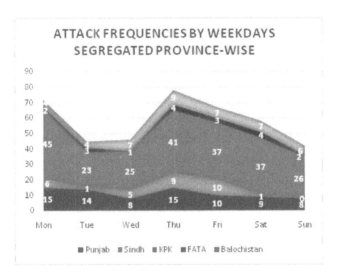

Figure. Weekly Frequency

# Attacks	Mon	Tue	Wed	Thu	Fri	Sat	Sun	Grand Total
Punjab	15	14	8	15	10	9	8	79
Sindh	6	1	5	9	10	1		32
KPK	45	23	25	41	37	37	26	234
FATA	2	3	1	4	3	4	2	19
Balochistan	4	4	7	9	7	7	6	44
Blanks	14	8	1	15	21	16	5	80
Grand Total	**86**	**53**	**47**	**93**	**88**	**74**	**47**	**488**

% Attacks	Mon	Tue	Wed	Thu	Fri	Sat	Sun	Grand Total
Punjab	18.99%	17.72%	10.13%	18.99%	12.66%	11.39%	10.13%	100.00%
Sindh	18.75%	3.13%	15.63%	28.13%	31.25%	3.13%	0.00%	100.00%
KPK	19.23%	9.83%	10.68%	17.52%	15.81%	15.81%	11.11%	100.00%
FATA	10.53%	15.79%	5.26%	21.05%	15.79%	21.05%	10.53%	100.00%
Balochistan	9.09%	9.09%	15.91%	20.45%	15.91%	15.91%	13.64%	100.00%
Blanks	17.50%	10.00%	1.25%	18.75%	26.25%	20.00%	6.25%	100.00%
Grand Total	**17.62%**	**10.86%**	**9.63%**	**19.06%**	**18.03%**	**15.16%**	**9.63%**	**100.00%**

Figure. Week for Provinces

The day of the week, thus, seems to be an important determinant of an attack. Thursday is most common for all provinces, and Friday for Sindh. Overall, Tuesdays, Wednesdays, and Sundays are lowest for all provinces. As seen from the graph above, all provinces show a homogenous pattern with respect to weekdays.

5.3. Attacks on Fridays killed most on average

On Fridays, we usually have crowds on roads in the afternoon due to the Friday prayers, which may be inferred to be the cause of the greater number of casualties on this day of the week.

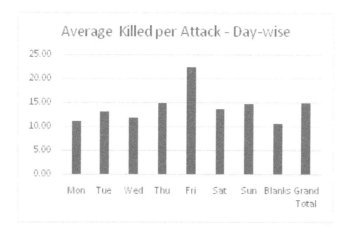

Figure. Average People Killed by Days

FATA has lowest casualties per attack, which probably owes to a lower population density[1] in the area as compared to other provinces. The population density of FATA as a whole is only 117 persons per square kilometer, while the population density of Punjab is 459. However, there is a wide variation between individual agencies and Frontier Regions (FRs). For example, in FR Dera Ismail Khan, the population is thinly scattered with 19 persons per square kilometer, while population density in Bajaur Agency reaches 461 persons per square kilometer[2].

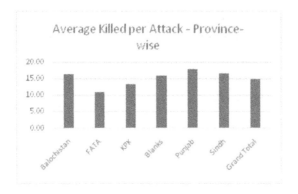

Figure. Average killed per Attack

Province	# Attacks	Killed_Max	# Foriegn.	%Gap between max/min killed/injured	Avg Killed per attack
Balochistan	44	713	0	25.18%	16.20
FATA	19	205	0		10.79
KPK	234	3110	7	34.46%	13.29
Blanks	80	1267	0	35.52%	15.84
Punjab	79	1405	5	31.97%	17.78
Sindh	32	527	12	32.46%	16.47
Grand Total	488	7227	24	33.62%	14.81

Figure. Province-wise Average killed per Attack

5.4. Attacks on Foreigners

Only seven attacks on foreigners have been identified so far, out of 488. In those seven attacks, a total of 84 fatalities occurred and from them, only 24 were foreigners, which is 28.57% of the total losses.

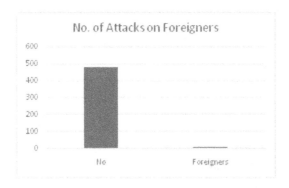

Figure. No. of Attacks on Foreigners

Foreigners (Y/N)	# Attacks	Killed_Max	# Foriegn.	%Gap between maximin killed/injured	Avg Killed per attack
No	481	7143	0	33.70%	14.85
Foreigners	7	84	24	29.85%	12.00
Grand Total	488	7227	24	33.62%	14.81

Figure. Grid-view of No. of Attacks on Foreigners

5.5. Number of bombers per attack

Mostly, the attacks were carried out by one bomber majorly in FATA, Baluchistan and KPK. However, a few attacks have also had multiple bombers. Punjab is more prone to attacks with multiple bombers as compared to other provinces. Only 73% attacks in Punjab were from single bomber as compared to 85% overall.

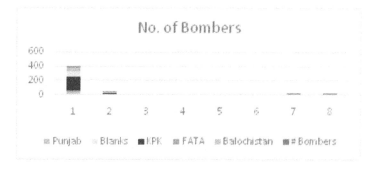

Figure. Number of Bombers

# Bombers	1	2	3	4	5	7	9	10
Balochistan	88.10%	9.52%	2.38%					
FATA	94.44%	5.56%						
KPK	86.40%	7.02%	2.63%	1.75%	1.75%	0.44%		
Blanks	89.74%	8.97%	1.28%					
Punjab	73.42%	16.46%	3.80%	1.27%	2.53%	1.27%	1.27%	
Sindh	77.42%	6.45%	6.45%		6.45%			3.23%
Grand Total	84.66%	9.03%	2.73%	1.05%	1.66%	0.42%	0.21%	0.21%

Figure. Grid-view of Number of Bombers Province-wise

5.6. Bomber Profiles

The age of the bomber ranges between 13 years to 33 years. The notable age range is teenagers between 12 and 22 years, the age when the zeal for life and life's responsibilities is at their peak among the youth. This is also the age when the youth in question can easily derive the basis of his decisions from emotions instead of cognitive logic. Moreover, at times, suicide bombers come with some additional weapons such as hand grenades, pistols and guns etc. In the employment of additional weapons, the use of hand grenades is only associated with attackers in their late teens.

Bomber Age	Hand Grenade	No Hand Grenade	Grand Total
13		1	1
14		2	2
15		12	12
16		7	7
17		13	13
18		10	10
19	1	7	8
20	1	14	15
21	1	5	6
22		5	5
23		4	4
24		4	4
25		1	1
28		3	3
30		4	4
33		2	2
(blank)	20	371	391
Grand Total	23	465	488

Figure. Bomber Age Profile

5.7. Number of Blasts and Casualties

On a single day, three suicide attacks have fewer casualties than two attacks, which could be due to precautionary measures taken by the public.

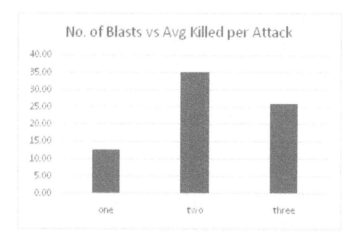

Figure. No. of Blast vs Average Killed per Attack

This also suggests that if terrorists were to carry out multiple attacks in a single day they are likely to harm fewer people as compared to conducting single attacks spread over different days. This also suggests that they are perhaps aware of this, an alarming reflection of their degree of sophistication and training. Most attacks involve one bomber are one-bombed, while less frequent are two and three-bombed and hardly any beyond three-bombs.

# Bombs	# Attacks	Killed_Max	# Foriegn.	%Gap between max/min killed/injured	Avg Killed per attack
one	425	5311	17	33.56%	12.50
two	37	1301	4	30.40%	35.16
three	11	285	3	38.97%	25.91
five	1	6	0		6.00
seven	1	148	0		148.00
(blank)	13	176	0	65.58%	13.54
Grand Total	488	7227	24	33.62%	14.81

Figure. Grid-view of Blast vs Average Killed

5.8. Attacks Claimed by Groups

Suicide bombers who came with additional weapons such as hand grenades have a higher probability of being followed by issuance of a statement from attackers:

HandGrenade Y/N	NoStatement	StatementGiven	Total
Yes	18	5	23
No	427	38	465
Grand Total	445	43	488

HandGrenade Y/N	NoStatement	StatementGiven	Total
Yes	78.26%	21.74%	100.00%
No	91.83%	8.17%	100.00%
Grand Total	91.19%	8.81%	100.00%

Figure. Hand Grenades with Statement

In order to test the statistical significance of the above claim that the use of hand grenades increases the probability of issuance of a statement, this study uses the Wilcoxon rank-sum test also known as Mann–Whitney U test[3], which is a non-parametric alternative to the group-wise t-test. Non-parametric tests are applicable when little or nothing is known about the population distribution and/or when sample sizes are very small. These don't make use of any assumptions about the data distribution, and instead rely on computational power through re-sampling. These tests weren't popular before advanced computational powers of modern statistical software. Thus our lack of knowledge about distributions can be compensated with computational power.

The p-value for Wilcoxon rank-sum test is 2.53%, meaning the attacks with and without hand grenades are statistically different from each other with regard to the probability of a statement being made afterwards. Other words, if grenade attacks weren't inherently associated with a higher probability of statements, then there would be only 2.53% chance of us observing the data that we are observing.

This suggests that suicide bombers who came with hand grenades, come from top tier leadership of terrorist organizations with a particular and specific motive which follows with the issuance of a statement. These attacks are thus more comprehensively planned and involve top leadership. Other attacks, in contrast, may have been ad hoc and come from ordinary lower rank members of these organizations without any specific motive other than their broad general manifesto.

Most attacks are unclaimed, which highlights two things. First, terrorist organizations don't have a central command and control. Attacks from renowned terrorist organizations are usually followed by a statement or at least a claim, and attacks that come from lower ranks don't come with any claim.

The poor command and control among terrorist organizations also makes it very hard for authorities to make any negotiations with them as there is no control on who will plan and launch an attack. It also highlights Pakistan's stance on foreign involvement. When most attacks are unclaimed, others can aide or conduct such attacks under the guise of local terrorists. Moreover, three out of seven attacks on foreigners have been claimed by the terrorist organizations.

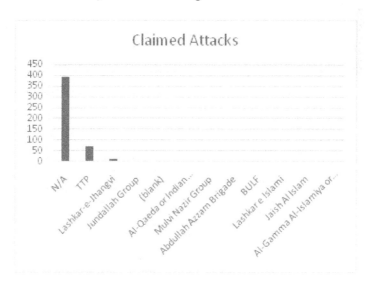

Figure. Claimed Attack

Claimed By:	No Foreigners	Foreigners	Grand Total
N/A	387	4	391
TTP	70	1	71
Lashkar-e-Jhangvi	12		12
Jundallah Group	4		4
(blank)	3		3
Al-Qaeda or Indian involvement		1	1
Mulvi Nazir Group	1		1
Abdullah Azzam Brigade	1		1
BULF	1		1
Lashkar e Islami	1		1
Jaish Al Islam	1		1
Al-Gamma Al-Islamiya or Party of Islam		1	1
Grand Total	481	7	488

Figure. Attacks on Foreigner Claimed by Organizations

5.9. Comparison of Tehreek Taliban Pakistan and Lashkar-e-Jhangvi

Tehreek Taliban Pakistan (TTP) and Lashkar-e-Jhangvi (LeJ) are the two main terrorist organizations that frequently claimed responsibility for suicide attacks afterwards. The highest no. of attacks have claimed by TTP. The TTP was mainly established to demolish the NATO/ISAF forces in Afghanistan but, as the Pakistan is providing the path of NATO supply to Afghanistan, it became another strong reason of TTP to being active in suicide attacks in the region.

Claimed By:	# Attacks	Killed_Max	# Foriegn.	%Gap between max/min killed/injured	Avg Killed per attack
Lashkar-e-Jhangvi	12	486	0	17.57%	40.50
TTP	71	1578	3	32.74%	22.23
Grand Total	83	2064	3	30.71%	24.87

Figure. Comparison of TTP and LeJ

LeJ executes deadlier attacks than TTP and kills twice number of people per attack than TTP. Figure below presents the details of the rate of those killed in claimed attacks.

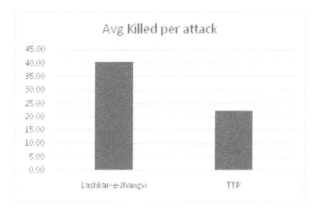

Figure. Average Killed Rate per Attack

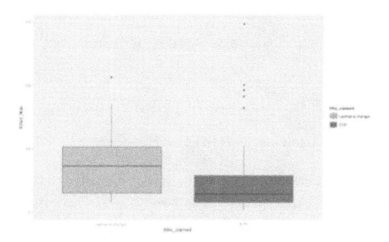

Figure. Who Claimed Attack Rate

The Wilcoxon test yields p-value of 1.03% indicating TTP and LeJ are statistically different from each other with regard to casualties per attack, as there is only 1.03% chance of observing this data if it weren't the case.

5.10. Execution of Sectarian Attacks

On average, sectarian attacks kill almost twice of the people per attack. In the above graph, it's proven that Lashkar-e-Jhangvi executes more lethal attack then TTP and kills twice no. of people per attack. Thus, it's also proven that LeJ execute only sectarian attacks.

Sectarian	# Attacks	Killed_Max	# Foriegn.	%Gap betwee	Avg Killed per attack
Non_Sectarian	429	5898	24	34.35%	13.75
Sectarian	55	1294	0	28.14%	23.53
(blank)	4	35	0	41.07%	8.75
Grand Total	488	7227	24	33.62%	14.81

Figure. Sectarian Attacks Killed Twice on Average

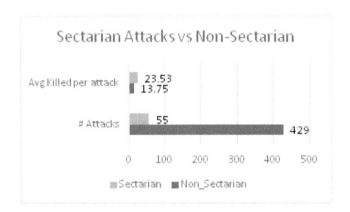

Figure. Sectarian Attacks vs Non-Sectarian

LeJ is an anti-Shiite terrorist organization and their motives are religious, so this makes it quite evident for sectarian attacks, and their extremism toward casualties' ratio per attack.

Claimed By:	Non_Sectarian	Sectarian	(blank)	Grand Total
Others	10	2	2	14
Lashkar-e-Jhangvi		12		12
N/A	352	37	2	391
TTP	67	4		71
Grand Total	429	55	4	488

Claimed By:	Non_Sectarian	Sectarian	(blank)	Grand Total
Others	71.43%	14.29%	14.29%	100.00%
Lashkar-e-Jhangvi	0.00%	100.00%	0.00%	100.00%
N/A	90.03%	9.46%	0.51%	100.00%
TTP	94.37%	5.63%	0.00%	100.00%
Grand Total	87.91%	11.27%	0.82%	100.00%

Figure. Sectarian Attacks by LeJ

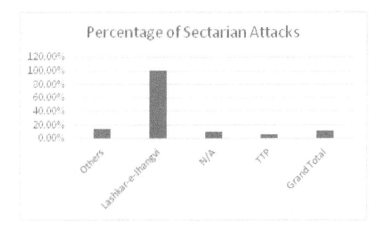

Figure. Percentage of Sectarian Attacks

However, further analysis shows that LeJ inherently executes deadlier attacks than TTP. In other words, sectarian attacks are not a confounding variable as seen from tables below. TTP has same average killed per attacks for both sectarian and other attacks. This implies that merely targeting a religious gathering, mosque or temple wouldn't automatically result in a greater number of casualties.

It is more likely that TTP has better trained attackers or more advanced bombs, further implying that sectarian attacks are not a significant factor and the mode of operation of LeJ is inherently different from TTP in some way that causes more casualties,

	# Attacks	Killed_Max	# Foriegn.	Avg Killed per attack
Others	14	312	15	22.29
Lashkar-e-Jhangvi	12	486	0	40.50
N/A	391	4851	6	12.41
TTP	71	1578	3	22.23
Grand Total	488	7227	24	14.81

	# Attacks	Killed_Max	# Foriegn.	Avg Killed per attack
Group1	2	64	0	32.00
Lashkar-e-Jhangvi	12	486	0	40.50
N/A	37	654	0	17.68
TTP	4	90	0	22.50
Grand Total	55	1294	0	23.53

Figure. Attacks by LeJ and TTP

73

Both TTP and LeJ groups still show same trend of attacks on weekdays except Friday.

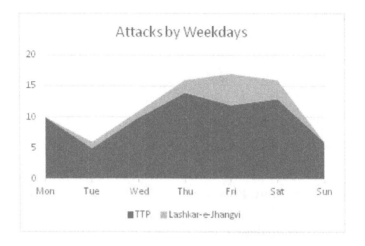

Figure. Attacks Frequency by LeJ and TTP

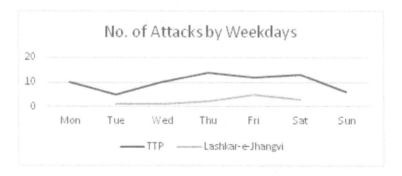

Figure. Trend of Attacks by LeJ and TTP

Thursdays and Fridays are highly preferred days for both organizations, Sundays and Tuesdays are at the least prefered by both. LeJ has never attacked on Mondays or Sundays whereas TTP has frequently attacked on Mondays.

LeJ mostly targets Baluchistan - 66.7% of all its attacks have taken place in Baluchistan. TTP hardly ever targets Baluchistan, but targets KPK more frequently as compared to other provinces.

Claimed By:	Punjab	Sindh	KPK	FATA	Balochistan	Blanks	Grand Total
N/A	69	22	186	19	31	64	391
TTP	7	8	40		2	14	71
Others	2	2	5		3	2	14
Lashkar-e-Jhangvi	1		3		8		12
Grand Total	79	32	234	19	44	80	488

Claimed By:	Punjab	Sindh	KPK	FATA	Balochistan	Blanks	Grand Total
N/A	17.85%	5.63%	47.57%	4.86%	7.93%	16.37%	100.00%
TTP	9.86%	11.27%	56.34%	0.00%	2.82%	19.72%	100.00%
Others	14.29%	14.29%	35.71%	0.00%	21.43%	14.29%	100.00%
Lashkar-e-Jhangvi	8.33%	0.00%	25.00%	0.00%	66.67%	0.00%	100.00%
Grand Total	16.19%	6.56%	47.95%	3.89%	9.02%	16.39%	100.00%

Figure. Terrorist Attacks in Provinces

LeJ is more involved in killings in Baluchistan and specifically the Hazara community as most of Hazara community lives in Quetta. The basic motives of LeJ are to constitute a team against the Shias. The primary target of the TTP, however, is to spread terror regardless of the location. Further, LeJ has also targeted Shia pilgrims on their journey towards Iran and Iraq via Baluchistan.

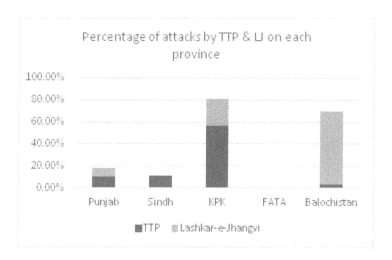

Figure. Percentage of Attacks by LeJ and TTP

TTP is much more likely to issue a statement after the attack i.e. 47.8% of its attacks entailed a statement whereas overall only 8.8% of the total number of attacks had a statement.

Attacker	NoStatement	StatementGiven	Grand Total
N/A	390	1	391
TTP	34	37	71
Others	10	4	14
Lashkar-e-Jhangvi	11	1	12
Grand Total	445	43	488

Attacker	NoStatement	StatementGiven	Grand Total
N/A	99.74%	0.26%	100.00%
TTP	47.89%	52.11%	100.00%
Others	71.43%	28.57%	100.00%
Lashkar-e-Jhangvi	91.67%	8.33%	100.00%
Grand Total	91.19%	8.81%	100.00%

Figure. Attackers Statement

The percentage of attacks that were followed by issuance of a statement by the group has been shown in "Attackers Statement".

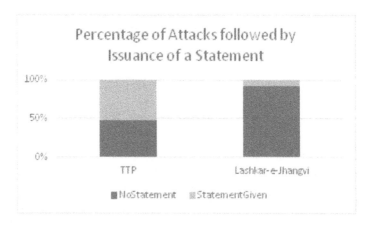

Figure. Percentage of Attacks followed by Issuance of a Statement

5.11. Attack Type

Attack Type for Foreigners represent the way suicide attacks have been conducted. Attacks on foreigners are well-planned and sophisticated and often involve vehicles, as represented in "Attack Type for Foreigners" and "Attack Mode by Terrorist Groups".

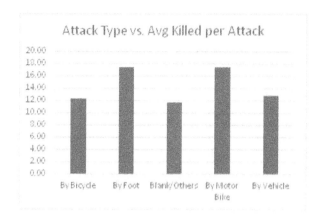

Figure. Attack Type vs. Average Killed per Attack

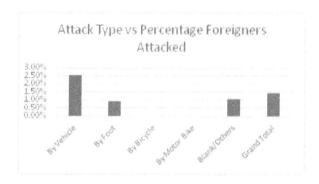

Figure. Attack Type for Foreigners

Bomb Type	No Foreigners	Foreigners	Grand Total
By Vehicle	155	4	159
By Foot	216	2	218
By Bicycle	3		3
By Motor Bike	16		16
Blank/Others	91	1	92
Grand Total	481	7	488

Bomb Type	No Foreigners	Foreigners	Grand Total
By Vehicle	97.48%	2.52%	100.00%
By Foot	99.08%	0.92%	100.00%
By Bicycle	100.00%	0.00%	100.00%
By Motor Bike	100.00%	0.00%	100.00%
Blank/Others	98.91%	1.09%	100.00%
Grand Total	98.57%	1.43%	100.00%

Figure. Attack Type for Foreigners

TTP and LeJ aren't much different with respect to the above mentioned attack types. Thus higher casualties of LeJ can be attributed to neither of those.

Attack Type	N/A	TTP	Others	Lashkar-e-	Grand Total
By Vehicle	123	26	5	5	159
By Foot	168	38	7	5	218
By Bicycle	3				3
By Motor Bike	15	1			16
Others	82	6	2	2	92
Grand Total	391	71	14	12	488

Attack Type	N/A	TTP	Others	Lashkar-e-	Grand Total
By Vehicle	31.46%	36.62%	35.71%	41.67%	32.58%
By Foot	42.97%	53.52%	50.00%	41.67%	44.67%
By Bicycle	0.77%	0.00%	0.00%	0.00%	0.61%
By Motor Bike	3.84%	1.41%	0.00%	0.00%	3.28%
Others	20.97%	8.45%	14.29%	16.67%	18.85%
Grand Total	100.00%	100.00%	100.00%	100.00%	100.00%

Figure. Attack Mode by Terrorist Groups

5.12. Relationship between Bomb Weight and Fatality Rate

Contrary to what one would expect, there emerges no significant correlation between bomb weight and the total number of individuals killed.

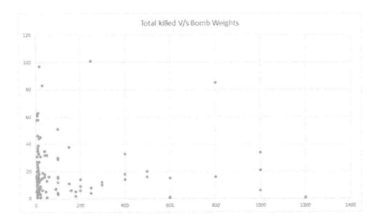

Figure. Total Killed vs Bomb Weights

5.13. Correlation Analysis of Suicide Bombing and Drone Attacks

Following is a chart that depicts the monthly frequency of suicide bombing and drones from Jan 2005 till March 2015. Both suicide attacks and drones were very rare till 2006. Suicide attacks increased tremendously during 2007-08 period, while there was no such increase in drones during or before this period. The frequency of drones only picked up in Sep 2008 onwards, while suicide attacks frequency remained the same till 2009 as it was in 2007-08. Drones then saw a sharp increase in the last quarter of 2010, after which the frequency of suicide attacks dropped to some extent. The frequency of drones then plummeted at the end of 2012 and in early 2013 while suicide attacks again increased in early 2013.

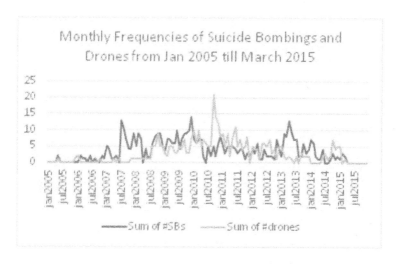

Figure. Monthly Frequency of Suicide Bombings and Drones

If we plot monthly frequency of suicide attacks and drones from Jan 2005 till March 2015 we get a Pearson's correlation of 23.9% and if we do the same thing on a quarterly basis rather than monthly for the same time period, we get Pearson's correlation of 30%. Monthly basis Correlation and Quarterly basis Correlation represent the Pearson's correlation for monthly and quarterly periods respectively.

Month	#SBs	#drones
jan2005	0	0
feb2005	0	0
mar2005	0	0
apr2005	0	0
may2005	2	1
....	....	....
sep2014	1	2
oct2014	3	7
nov2014	1	4
dec2014	2	5
jan2015	1	5
feb2015	3	0
mar2015	2	1

Qtr	#SBs	#drones
2005Q1	0	0
2005Q2	2	1
2005Q3	0	0
2005Q4	0	1
2006Q1	3	2
2006Q2	3	0
2006Q3	1	0
2006Q4	3	1
2007Q1	10	0
....	....	....
2013Q1	19	8
2013Q2	29	3
2013Q3	11	5
2013Q4	13	6
2014Q1	15	0
2014Q2	6	2
2014Q3	1	6
2014Q4	6	16
2015Q1	6	6

Figure. Monthly basis Correlation & Quarterly basis Correlation

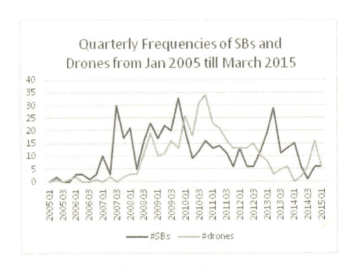

Figure. Quarterly Frequencies of Suicide Bombings and Drones

The quarterly chart shows the same story i.e. suicide Bombings picked up much before Drones and there isn't much correlation between the two. However as we note, the granularity of time period effects the correlation. If we take 6 monthly or annual time periods we will see higher correlation. However from the graphs it appears that monthly/quarterly time frames are appropriate.

Notes

1 "Population by Gender (FATA)", Government of Khyber Pakhtunkhwa Finance Department, accessed April 20, 2015, http://financekpp.gov.pk/FD/kpk-at-a-glance/population-by-gender-fata.html

2 Ibid.

3 "Mann–Whitney *U* test", Wikipedia, accessed April 21, 2015, https://en.wikipedia.org/wiki/Mann%E2%80%93Whitney_U_test

4 "Map showing NATO supply routes through Pakistan," Wikipedia, accessed April 20, 2015, https://en.wikipedia.org/wiki/NATO_logistics_in_the_Afghan_War#/media/File:NATO_supply_routes_through_Pakistan.svg

6. Advanced Statistical Models for Forecasting

The goal of this chapter is to classify, evaluate and explore the statistical models that can help in the forecasting of suicide attacks.

> "I have seen the future and it is very much like the present, only longer."
>
> ~Kehlog Albran

In statistics, probability theory is used to analyze random phenomena. It is essential to many human activities that involve quantitative analysis of large sets of data.[1] Probability is a term that describes the measure of the chance of an event that may occur. It quantifies as a number between 0 and 1 (where 0 indicates impossibility, and 1 indicates certainty).[2] Conditional probability is one of the most important, and fundamental concepts in probability theory. It measures the probability of an event given that (by assumption, presumption, assertion or evidence) another event has occurred.[3]

6.1. Decision Tree Learning

The decision tree helps in the selection of statistics or statistical techniques appropriate to the purpose and conditions of a particular analysis. It is a powerful, yet simple form of analysis of multiple variables. It is a simple representation for classifying examples and provides distinct capabilities such as the following:[4]

- Traditional forms of statistical analysis like multilevel models
- Various data mining techniques like artificial neural networks

Algorithms produce decision trees. It identifies various ways of splitting a data set into branch-like segments. These segments form an inverted decision tree that originates with a root node at the top of the tree.[5] The main objective of a decision tree is to build a predictive model that predicts the value of a selected variable based on several input variables.[6]

6.2. Conditional Inference Tree

The Conditional Inference Tree is a type of decision tree learning method. In more technical term, it is known as *Unbiased Recursive Partitioning: A Conditional Inference Framework.*[7] Conditional inference trees estimate a regression relationship by binary recursive partitioning in a conditional inference framework. This approach uses non-parametric regression tests as splitting criteria, corrected for multiple testing to avoid over-fitting. It results in unbiased predictor selection and does not require pruning.[8]

Following are the steps a conditional inference tree algorithm usually follows: [9]

1. Test the global null hypothesis of independence between any of the input variables and the response (which may be multivariate as well). Stop if this hypothesis cannot be rejected. Otherwise select the input variable with the strongest association to the response. This association is measured by a p-value corresponding to a test for the partial null hypothesis of a single input variable and the response.
2. It implements a binary split on the nominated input variables.
3. Repeat steps 1 and 2, recursively.

The conditional inference tree is also used for predictive analysis in statistics. This technique has also been used in this research for predictive analysis because this single algorithm covers the following statistical methods: Factor Analysis, Variable Selection, Multilevel Regression, Conditional Probability (Permutation Tests, Multiple Testing), and Decision Tress (Ordinal Regression Trees, Multivariate Regression Trees) and generates tree visualizations for analysis.

6.3. Factors Analysis for Forecasting

6.3.1. Attacks on Armed Forces

The 'Primary Target' in data was used to assign a binary variable with '1' if any of the following categories were present Army/FC/Paramilitary/Security Forces/PAF. Total of 101 attacks (21%) had one of these i.e. they were on security forces or the army (excluded police). The main factor associated with such attacks is 'City'.

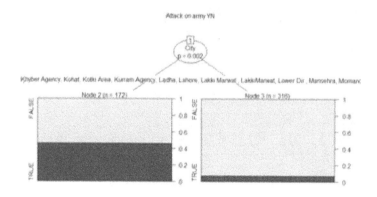

Figure. Primary Attack on Forces

The p-value is showing the significance of node 2 as it is less than 0.05. Node 2 has 46% attacks on armed forces vs. 21% overall; whereas node 3 has 7% attacks on armed forces.

It consists of 172 observations and include the following cities: Asad Khel, Attock, Bajaur, Bannu, Bara, Darra Adamkhel, Haripur, Jandola, Jandola Area, Karachi, Kharian, Landi Kotal, Malakand, Mardan, Mingora, Mirali, Miramshah, Miranshah, Mohmand Agency, Muzaffarabad, North Waziristan, Nowshera, Old Bara Area, Rawalakot, Rawalpindi, Sargodha, Sawat, Shabqadar, South Waziristan, SouthWaziristan, Swat, Tank, Tarar Khel and Wana.

Node 3 contains the remaining 316 observations and has only 7% attacks under the armed forces category. Thus, using just cities, we can divide the data into 46% vs. only 7%. It consists of following cities: Bajaur Agency, Balakot, Battagram District, Buner, Chakwal, Chaman, Charsadda, D.I Khan, Dargai, Dera Ghazi Khan, Dera Ismail Khan, Dir Bala, Ghundai Area, Gujrat, Hango, Hangu, Hub, Islamabad, Jamrud, Jhal Magsi, Kalat, Kamra, Karachi, Karak, Khanewal, Khar, Khyber Agency, Kohat, Kotki Area, Kurram Agency, Ladha, Lahore, Lakki Marwat, LakkiMarwat, Lower Dir, Mansehra, Momand Agency, Multan, Orakzai Agency, Parachinar, Parachinar, peshawar, Peshawar, Pishin, Qrakzai Agency, Quetta, Quetta, Shagla, Shakai Village, Shangla, Shikarpur, Sialkot, South Wazirisatn, Sukkur, Swabi, Tatalai, Taunsa Sharif, Thall, Tira, Khyber Agency, Tirah Valley, Upper Dir, Wah Cantt and Zhob.

6.3.2. Attacks on Police

The 'Primary Target' in the data was used to assign a binary variable with '1' if the attack was aimed at the police. 77 out of 488 attacks were targeted to the police, i.e. 16% of the total. Attacks on police mainly occurred in KPK and Sindh and had fewer casualties than other attacks. The following tree uses just the Province variable and whether or not if casualties in attack were less than 47 to classify attacks on police.

Node 3 has 32% attacks on police whereas nodes 4 and 5 have just 8% and 5% respectively, thus this signifies a huge difference.

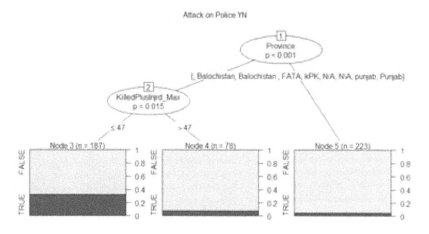

Figure. Primary Attack on Police

6.3.3. Attacks by Tehreek-e-Taliban Pakistan

The main predictor for TTP attacks is the issuance of a statement. 86% of attacks with statements were from TTP in node 2.

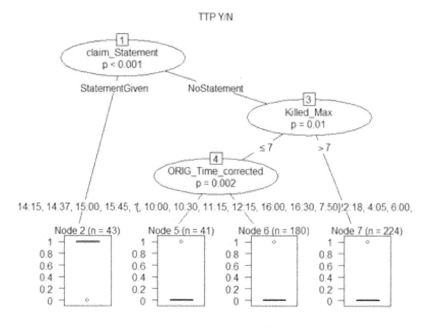

Figure. Claims of Attacks by TTP

6.3.4. Attacks by Lashkar-e-Jhangvi

The main predictor for LeJ is whether or not it was a sectarian attack. Node 2 with sectarian attacks has 22% attacks from LeJ whereas overall only 2.4% attacks are from LeJ.

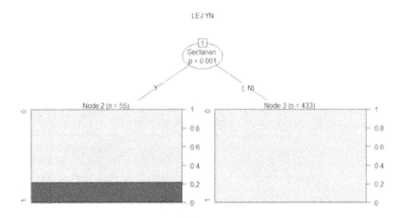

Figure. Claims of Attacks by LeJ

6.3.5. Sectarian Attacks

55 attacks were sectarian attacks that are 11.3% of total number of attacks. 12 of these attacks were perpetrated by LeJ. The following tree was formulated by excluding the attacker variable to see what other variable associates with sectarian attacks. Other variables include Weapons used and Time. It is observed that after 3 P.M. is a more likely time for sectarian attacks. Node 5 has 7% sectarian attacks that are 24/346 and node 6 has 16.6% sectarian that is 5/30. The proportion doubles with just the time factor with a p value of less than 4%.

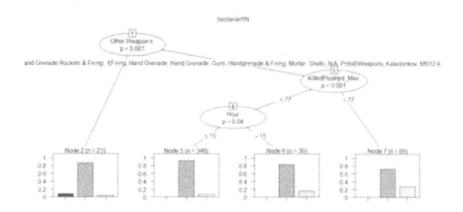

Figure. Sectarian Attacks

TTP attacks more during early hours and LeJ preferred times of attacks is after 3 P.M.

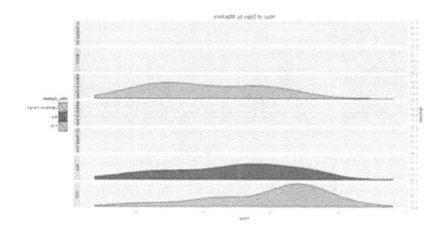

Figure. Time of Attacks by Claimed Groups

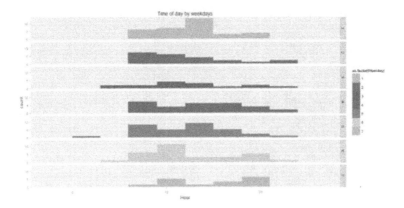

Figure. Comparison of Time by Weekdays

6.3.6. Statements Issued

A total of 43 attacks (8.8%) were followed up by statements from terrorist organizations. The main factor here is the claimers of attacks. Node 2 shows that terrorist groups like Jaish Al Islam, Jundallah Group and TTP had 79 attacks combined out of which 41 had statements i.e. 52% as compared to 8.8% overall. It covers 41 out of 43 attacks with statements. Node 3 shows that remaining terrorist groups like Abdullah Azzam Brigade, Al-Gamma Al-Islamiya or Party of Islam, Al-Qaeda or Indian involvement, BULF, Lashkar-e-Jhangvi, Lashkar e Islami, Mulvi Nazir Group, and undefined group issued just two statements out of the 409 attacks carried out by them.

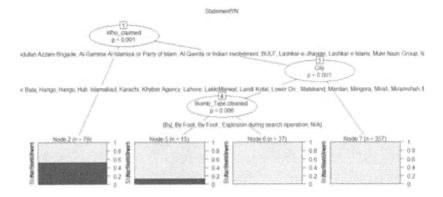

Figure. Statements Issued

6.4. Prediction Accuracy

A good model's selection criterion is an accuracy rate of over 70%. This study has tested the prediction accuracy on three data split-sets by using the Conditional Inference Tree.

1. 90% Training – 10 % Test data
2. 80% Training – 20 % Test data
3. 70% Training – 30 % Test data (minimum requirement standard for prediction)

The first three cases from the above section has been cross validated in this section. Remaining three cases: Attacks by LeJ, Sectarian Attacks and Statements Issued have been excluded because their sample size was not sufficient to perform the cross validation.

6.4.1. If Intended Target was the Armed Force, If Attack Foiled

According to the first split set 1, we get the training tree. Its overall accuracy is 69.4%, but 10% army attacks correctly classified.

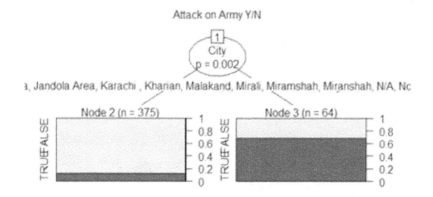

Figure. Split set 1 - Training Set of Armed Force Targets

	FALSE	TRUE
FALSE	33	6
TRUE	9	1

Table. Split set 1 – Test Results of Armed Force Targets

According to second split set, 67% accuracy has been achieved overall and only 25% of army attacks have been correctly identified.

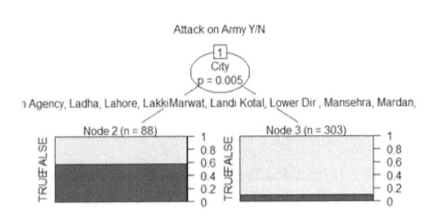

Figure. Split set 2- Training Set of Armed Force Targets

	FALSE	TRUE
FALSE	60	17
TRUE	15	5

Table. Split set 2 – Test Results of Armed Force Targets

According to third split set, an overall accuracy of 71.2% has been achieved. It correctly classifies 23.3% of attacks on armed forces and correctly classifies 83.6% of non-armed forces attacks.

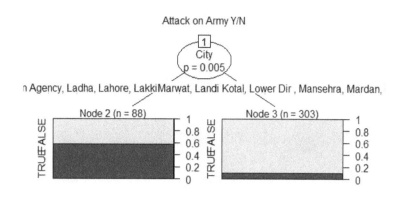

Figure. Split set 3 - Training Set of Armed Force Targets

	FALSE	**TRUE**
FALSE	97	19
TRUE	23	7

Table. Split set 3 – Test Results of Armed Force Targets

The overall accuracy rate of all three data split set has been provided in the table below. Accuracy is least with 90% split for this scenario. Below 70% accuracy rate of split sets will disqualify the model.

Data Split Set	*Accuracy Rate*
Split Set 1	69.4%
Split Set 2	67.0%
Split Set 3	71.2%

Table. Accuracy Rate of Split Sets for Armed Force Targets

6.4.2.   If Attack is on Police

According to first split set, following is the tree of training dataset. Overall accuracy rate is 67.3% and accuracy rate of attacks on police is 75% in node 4.

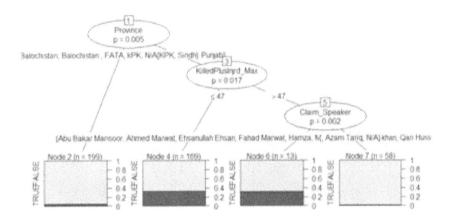

Figure. Split set 1 - Training Set of Attack on Police

	2	**4**	**6**	**7**
FALSE	23	12	2	4
TRUE	1	6	0	1

Table. Split set 1 – Test Results of Attack on Police

According to the second split set 2, the overall accuracy of the test set is 70.1% and only 60% of police attacks are classified correctly i.e. 9/15 of node 3.

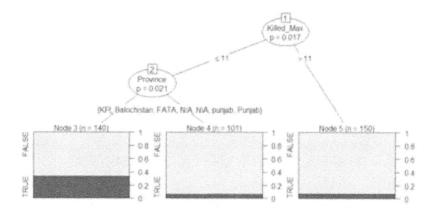

Figure. Split set 2 - Training Set of Attack on Police

	3	4	5
FALSE	23	29	30
TRUE	9	2	4

Table. Split set 2 – Test Results of Attack on Police

According to third split set 3, the tree of training dataset is depicted in figure below.

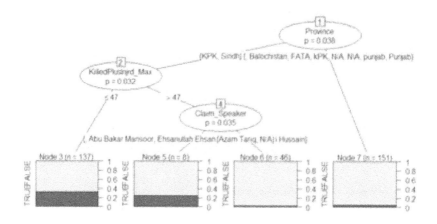

Figure. Split set 3 - Training Set of Attack on Police

	3	**5**	**6**	**7**
FALSE	34	7	15	67
TRUE	16	2	1	4

Table. Split set 3 – Test Results of Attack on Police

The overall accuracy rate is 37.4%. If we classify nodes 3 & 5 as attacks on police we will have correctly classified 78.3% of attacks on police and 71.5% of non-police attacks. Thus, the third split set gives best accuracy rate with 78% of police attacks correctly identified in test set. So partially, this split set is also accepted.

Data Split Set	*Accuracy Rate*
Split Set 1	67.3%
Split Set 2	70.1%
Split Set 3	37.4%

Table. Accuracy Rate of Split Sets for Attack on Police

Thus, several parameters have been discussed in terms of prediction and the accuracy results of test set prediction has also been underlined in detail. In a similar way, we are also enabled to predict the suicide attacks. However, predicting a suicide attack requires a more detailed analysis in order to come up with the finest fit of the algorithm(s). Analysis cum prediction are highly dependent on the understanding of data at first and at most on data cleaning.

6.4.3. If Attack by Tehreek-e-Taliban Pakistan

There are 71 attacks from Tehreek-e-Taliban Pakistan out of 488 total attacks i.e. 14.5%. According to first split-set, it will have 49 observations in the test set with 7 attacks of TTP, and 439 observations in the training set out of which 64 attacks are by TTP.

Using the training data to plot a tree only uses the claim statement variable for partitioning out of the following variables:

Formula = TTP ~ RareWeapons + Killed_Max + Injured_Max + KilledPlusInjrd_Max + City + Province + ORIG_Time_corrected + Weekday + No_of_Bombers + Bomber_susp_Age + Bomber_Origin. Identity + Bomb_Type.cleaned. + Bomb_Weight.kg + No_of_Bmbs + No.of.Foriegn. + Primary.Target + Sectarian.+ Religious. + claim_ Statement + Foreigners.Y.N. + count222 + Time_correctedaaa + Hour + HourBucket + lat + lon

For first split set, the tree shown below has been generated.

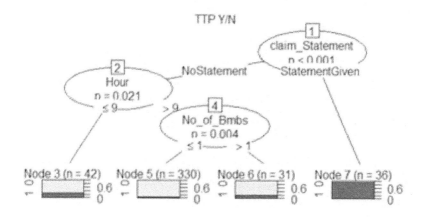

Figure. Split set 1 - Training Set of Attack by TTP

	0	1
0	40	2
1	2	5

Table. Split set 1 – Test Results of Attack by TTP

The figure above represents the results of the test set. It correctly identifies 5 out 7 TTP attacks i.e. 71.4% and it also correctly identifies

40 out of 42 non-TTP attacks i.e. 95.2%. Overall accuracy is 91.8% with a simple model. Thus we can use just the data to identify an attacker.

Changing the training and testing split percentage has a lot of impact on test set accuracy. For example, according to second split set we get the graphs of training set tree and test set results shown below. The overall accuracy is 90.7% but, here it identifies only 50% of TTP attacks correctly.

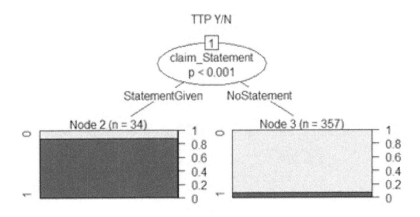

Figure. Split set 2 - Training Set of Attack by TTP

	0	1
0	81	2
1	7	7

Table. Split set 2 – Test Results of Attack by TTP

Reducing training set to 70% (split set 3) reduces accuracy even further for TTP attacks though all three models give us the very same tree and predictive function. The overall accuracy is 89.7% but only 38% TTP attacks were identified correctly.

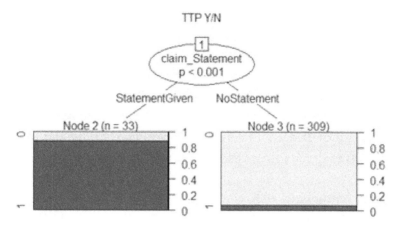

Figure. Split set 3 - Training Set of Attack by TTP

	0	1
0	123	2
1	13	8

Table. Split set 3 – Test Results of Attack by TTP

Data Split Set	*Accuracy Rate*
Split Set 1	91.8%
Split Set 2	90.7%
Split Set 3	89.7%

Table. Accuracy Rate of Split Sets for TTP Attack

6.5. Limitations

This chapter covered the advanced statistical inferential to give an overview of how it helps in forecasting with the dataset of suicide terrorism. There are few limitations of statistical models in making predictions. The predictive model highly depends on the type of data and the type of variable that we need to predict. Statistical models help with quantitative data type only. When it comes to ordinal and date types of data, one needs to explore other interdisciplinary branches of the statistic. There are two fields, Data Mining and Machine Learning, which provide a broad range of algorithms to understand and extract the kin and kith of dataset. They help in exploring, learning and training the models to predict the phenomena for the near future.

Machine learning is one of the subfields of computer science. It developed from the study of pattern recognition and computational learning theory in artificial intelligence.[10] It can learn from data and make predictions by exploring the construction and study of algorithms. Machine learning algorithms operate by building a model from example inputs to make data-driven predictions or decisions.[11]

Statistics and Machine learning are intimately related fields. Michael I. Jordan said that the idea of machine learning, from methodological principles to theoretical tools, have had a long pre-history in statistics. He suggested the term *"Data Science"*[12] as a place holding nomenclature for the overall field.[13]

Data Mining and Machine Learning starts where Statistics Inferential ends, but Data Science covers the fields overall. The researcher will explore, learn and implement these two domains in her advanced research concerning the phenomena of suicide attacks.

Notes

1   Probability Theory, Wikipedia, accessed June 7, 2015, http://en.wikipedia.org/wiki/Probability_theory.
2   Probability, Wikipedia, accessed June 7, 2015, http://en.wikipedia.org/wiki/Probability.

3   Conditional Probability, Wikipedia, accessed June 7, 2015, http://en.wikipedia. org/wiki/Conditional_probability.

4   "Decision Trees-What are they?" SAS, the power to know, accessed June 5, 2015, http://support.sas.com/publishing/pubcat/chaps/57587.pdf.

5   Ibid.

6   Decision Tree Learning, Wikipedia, accessed June 6, 2015, http://en.wikipedia. org/wiki/Decision_tree_learning.

7   Torsten Hothorm, Kurt Hornik and Achim Zeileis, "Unbiased Recursive Partitioning: A Conditional Inference Framework," Journal of Computational and Graphical Statistics, Volume 15, Number 3, Pages 651–674.

8   Conditional Inference Tress, Decision Tree Learning, Wikipedia, accessed June 6, 2015, http://en.wikipedia.org/wiki/Decision_tree_learning.

9   Conditional Inference Trees {party}, Inside-R, accessed June 6, 2015, http:// www.inside-r.org/packages/cran/party/docs/ctree.

10 Another domain of Computer Science in which scientist elastic enough power to machine to think.

11 Machine Learning, Wikipedia, accessed June 7, 2015, http://en.wikipedia.org/ wiki/Machine_learning.

12 Data Science is the extraction of knowledge from large volumes of data that aren't structured, which a continuation of the field data mining and predictive analytics, also known as knowledge discovery and data mining (KDD). "Unstructured data" can include emails, videos, photos, social media, and other user-generated content.

13 Machine Learning, Wikipedia, accessed June 7, 2015, http://en.wikipedia.org/ wiki/Machine_learning.

7. Conclusion

During recent years, Pakistan remained one of the country's worst-hit by suicide terrorism. According to the collected data that have been discussed in chapter 3, 22,553 fatalities occurred in just 488 attacks. The main goals of this research were to formulate a comprehensive dataset of suicide attacks; to analyze the dataset to identify patterns and to explore advance statistical models that can help in the forecasting of suicide attacks.

The motivation theories used in conducting this research were vengeance and personal traumatization. This study tested the hypothesis that; Pakistan faces suicide attack after each drone attack in Federally Administered Tribal Areas. The loss of family member(s), the loss of possessions or the long-term recovery process may lead the victims to set objectives for revenge from the government of Pakistan and Armed Forces. In order to analyze this hypothesis, the dataset of suicide bombing has been gathered to perform statistical analysis and to find out the correlation between suicide bombing and drone attacks. However, the hypothesis has been nullified by analysis of the data, as discussed in chapter 5.

The evolution of the concept of suicide bombing has been discussed in detail by finding its trails back in late 19th century in Russia. It was one of the favored terrorist tactics used in wars to create fear and disturbance. After that, the first incident happened during the Israeli occupation in Lebanon. Pakistan faced its first suicide attack in 1995 in the capital Islamabad at the Egyptian embassy. The summary of province-wise suicide attacks and high-profile attacks in terms of high fatality rate, major primary target, have been underlined and stated that Peshawar, Khyber Pakhtunkha is the primary target of suicide bombers. The Tehreek–e-Taliban Pakistan (TTP) and Lashkar-e-Jhangvi (LeJ) are two main militant bodies who are actively participating in spreading the terror of suicide attacks. Both groups have their strong roots in Khyber Pakhtunkha.

The study of terrorist groups that are present in the territory of Pakistan; and actively or partially involved in suicide attacks provides a good understanding about their landscape, motives and their links with other local and international terrorist organizations.

The first objective of the study was to formulate a comprehensive dataset of suicide bombing in Pakistan. An extensive study has been conducted on the existing terrorism dataset and specifically suicide bombing dataset by the national and international organizations. Pakistan lacks an institute that monitors and maintain the detailed statistics on suicide bombing ground. However, a new comprehensive database has been formulated, which serves to be a most authentic database of suicide bombing in Pakistan. This database records and covers all suicide bombing news via printed and electronic media. Various other variables were also discussed that could be incorporated in the current database to make it more comprehensive. It can only be possible by establishing a counter-terrorism organization in Pakistan who has rights to maintain and cover each aspect of a suicide attack. Such practice will set a benchmark on the existing datasets of terrorism.

The second objective was to analyze the dataset to find useful insights about suicide attacks. After the formulation of the suicide bombing dataset, an in-depth quantitative analysis has been performed. Quantitative methods are ideally applicable to find out the key questions: who, what, when and where. The following useful insights have been discovered from the data:

- Khyber Pakhtunkhwa is the most frequently attacked province with the highest number of causalities.
- Peshawar faced the highest number of attacks and Quetta faced the second highest.
- Both, Peshawar and Quetta are the gateways of NATO supply to Afghanistan.
- The average rate of casualties per attack is high in Punjab because of population density.
- The year 2009 and 2013 were the deadliest years in the history of Khyber Pakhtunkhwa
- Attacks increased in the year 2007. In the same year, Lal Masjid incident occurred, and the terrorist organization TTP was established.
- Thursday is the most likely day of attack.
- Friday is the most likely day of attack for Sindh.
- The fatality rate, as compared to other weekdays, is high in Friday attacks.
- Punjab, Sindh, and Khyber Pakhtunkha are most likely to face more than two suicide attacks in a single day.
- A total of seven attacks have targeted foreigners; these caused 84 fatalities in total and from them only 28.57% were foreigners.
- LeJ kills twice number of people per attack than TTP.
- LeJ executes only sectarian attacks, kills twice as many people as compared to non-sectarian attacks.
- TTP and LeJ are most likely to attack on Thursday and Friday; and Sunday and Tuesday are at their least preferred weekdays.
- LeJ never attacks on Monday or Sunday.
- LeJ's preferred time to attack is after 3 P.M.
- LeJ is more likely to be involved in Baluchistan and specifically targets the Hazara community.
- TTP is more likely to attack during the early hours between 5 A.M. to 11 A.M.
- TTP is more involved in attacks in Khyber Pakhtunkha province.

- TTP is much more likely to issue a statement after the attack i.e. 47.8% of its attacks entailed a statement
- Attacks on foreigners are well-planned and often involve vehicles.
- **No Correlation has found between drone attacks and suicide bombing.**

Moreover, if we link the stats of data with the timeline of social and political factors and transitions, it will more comprehensively help to relate the causes and causations between incidents of attacks.

The final objective was to explore the statistical models that can help in forecasting. In advanced statistical models, conditional inferential tree algorithm has been explored. This single algorithm comes with different statistical functions to perform and generate decision trees in the end. The most empowering function of conditional tree is factor analysis, which identifies the significant variables from the dataset. Prediction model has been trained and cross validated on 3 sets of data splits. More than 70% accuracy has been achieved, which is acceptable.

In the current research, a most authentic dataset of suicide bombing has been established, on which data analysis and advanced statistical inferential analysis was performed for the purpose of forecasting. The research has covered the most useful and appropriate statistical methods that can help in prediction. This research is limited to advances in statistical analysis and it also classifies that statistics and advanced statistical models can be applied on any social phenomena in order to identify any hidden existing patterns and forecast future trends.

Data Mining and Machine Learning are the fields using which the researcher can perform prediction on the data of random phenomena. These fields provide a large range of algorithms that can learn from data and built a model to make predictions of future trends. Both fields are closely linked with Statistics and Computer Science.

7.1.   Future Directions

For future directions, researchers can work in the following domains:

- Enhancement of existing datasets with the variables discussed in Chapter 3.
- Explore the fields of Data Mining and Machine Learning.
- Conduct exploratory research on how statistical analysis can use for forecasting.
- Find the causes and causations by correlating the timeline of suicide attacks with the social and political factors.

7.2.   Recommendations

A few recommendations have been discussed here by stating the case study of RAND Corporation.

The RAND Corporation is a U.S. based research organization that helps in developing solutions to improve public policy and decision-making through "research and analysis", to make communities safer, secure and more prosperous. The corporation aim is to solve the world's pressing challenges, by covering the wide range of research domains i.e. National Security, Health and Wellness Promotion, Counterterrorism, Water Resources Management, Drug Policy and Trends, to name a few.

It was observed that such organizations have a multi-disciplinary team[1] because there is a point where every person needs to work together. A computer scientist may be able to develop a solution alone but can't implement it in society. Together with the multi-disciplinary team, the designed solution can more easily be implemented with common understanding and collaboration.

RAND Corporation is a good example from which to learn. We should establish a counter-terrorism organization in Pakistan with the collaboration of National ICT Research and Development funds, Innovation Development Fund (an initiative of the government of Punjab). In Pakistan, research and development needs to be promoted in order to stand and compete with international organizations. It will also help the students, researches, professors, professionals and industry experts of different domains to unify and integrate at a single place to settle down the issue from its root causes. At most, it helps to figure out the eruption of syndromes at their early stage and to propose possible solutions and improve public policies and the decision-making process.

Notes

1   "RAND at a Glance," RAND Corporation, http://www.rand.org/about/glance. html.

References

Books

Charny, I. W. *Fighting suicide bombing: A World wide campaign for life.* Connecticut: Praeger Security International, 2007.

Electronic Statistics Textbook. Tulsa, OK: StatSoft, 2013. http://www.statsoft.com/textbook/.

Hafez, Mohammed. *Suicide Bomber in Iraq: The Strategy and ideology of Martyrdom.* Washington, DC: United States Institute of Peace, 2007

Merari, Ariel. *Driven to death: Psychological and social aspects of suicide terrorism.* New York: Oxford University Press, Inc., 2010.

Murphy, Eamon. *The Making of Terrorism in Pakistan: Historical and Social Roots of Extremism.* Oxon and New York: Routledge Critical Terrorism Studies, 2013.

Pape, Robert. *Dying to Win: The Strategic Logic of Suicide Terrorism.* New York: Random House, 2005.

RAND Corporation. *Predicting Suicide Attacks - Integrating Spatial, Temporal, and Social Features of Terrorist Attack Targets.* Santa Monica, CA: RAND Corporation, 2013.

Skaine, Rosemarie. *Suicide Warfare – Culture, the Military and the Individual as a Weapon*. California: Library of Congress Cataloging-in-Publication Data, 2013.

Journal Articles

Hassan, Riaz. "What motivated the suicide bombers?." *Yale Global Online Magazine*, September 3, 2009. Accessed August 21, 2014. http://yaleglobal.yale.edu/print/5926.

Lankford, Adam. "Requirements and Facilitators for Suicide Terrorism: an Explanatory Framework for Prediction and Prevention," *Perspective on Terrorism* 5, no. 5-6 (2011). Accessed May 21, 2015. http://www.terrorismanalysts.com/pt/index.php/pot/article/view/requirements-and-facilitators/html.

Lewis, Jeffrey W. "The Human Use of Human Beings: A Brief History of Suicide Bombing," *Origins - Current Events in Historical Perspective* 6, no. 7 (2013). Accessed May 19, 2015. http://origins.osu.edu/article/human-use-human-beings-brief-history-suicide-bombing.

Michael, Sabir. "Terrorism a Socio-Economic and Political Phenomenon with Special Reference to Pakistan." *Journal of Management and Social Sciences* 3, no. 1 (Spring 2007)

Mickolus, Edward F. et al. "International Terrorism: Attributes of Terrorist Events." Dunn Loring, VA: Vinyard Software, 2006.

Moghadam, Assaf. "Shifting Trends in Suicide Attacks," *Combating Terrorism Center Sentinel* 2, no. 1 (2009): 11-13.

Schweitze, Yoram. "Istishad as an ideological and practical tool in the hands of Al- Qaeda," *Journal of National Defense Studies*, no. 6 (2008): 113-137.

Venables, W. N, Smith, D. M, and the R Core Team. "An Introduction to R."

Newspaper Reports

Hairan, Abdulhadi. "The History of Suicide Attacks in Pakistan." Ground Report, 2007. Accessed May 10, 2015. http://groundreport. com/the-history-of-suicide-attacks-in-pakistan/.

Leger, Donna, Johnson, Kevin, Stanglin, Doug. "Boston bombs were pressure cookers filled with metal." USA Today. Accessed March 21, 2015. http://www.usatoday.com/story/news/nation/2013/04/16/ boston-marathon-explosions/2086853/.

Think-Tank Reports

Bomb Data Center, FBI. "Improvised Explosive Devices Used in Suicide Bombing Incidents." Public Intelligence. Accessed March 23, 2015. https://info.publicintelligence.net/bombcenteried.pdf.

"Chicago Project on Security and Terrorism (CPOST)." Suicide Attack Database. UChicago CPOST.

Dodd, Henry. "A short history of suicide bombing." *Action on Armed Violence*, Aug 23, 2013. Accessed May 9, 2015. https://aoav.org. uk/2013/a-short-history-of-suicide-bombings/.

Institute for conflict management. "South Asia Terrorism Portal (SATP)."

National Consortium for the Study of Terrorism And Responses to Terrorism (START). "Global Terrorism Database (GTD)."

Pak Institute of Peace Studies. "Pak Institute of Peace Studies, Independent Think-Tank in Pakistan." Accessed on April 3, 2015. http://san-pips.com/.

"Preparation of a Suicide Bomber." The Mechanics of a Living Bombs. War Online. Accessed March 23, 2015. http://www.waronline.org/en/terror/suicide.htm

"RAND database of Worldwide Terrorism Incidents (RDWTI)." RAND Corporation.

"Suicide Bombing." Pakistan Body Count. http://pakistanbodycount.org/suicide_bombing.

Miscellaneous

James Kiras, Kames. "Suicide Bombing," Encyclopedia Britannica. Aug 07, 2014. Accessed May 9, 2015, http://www.britannica.com/EBchecked/topic/736115/suicide-bombing.

"Mapping Militant Organizations." Stanford University. http://web.stanford.edu/group/mappingmilitants/cgi-bin

Appendix

Suicide Bombing in Pakistan dataset till December 2015 is attached.

No	Date of Attack	Killed		Injurd	
		Min	Max	Min	Max
1	Saturday, November 18, 1995		16		60
2	Monday, November 6, 2000		3		3
3	Wednesday, May 8, 2002		16		20
4	Friday, June 14, 2002		13		51
5	Friday, July 4, 2003	44	47	65	70
6	Sunday, December 14, 2003		0		0
7	Thursday, December 25, 2003		18		50
8	Saturday, February 28, 2004		1	3	4
9	Friday, May 7, 2004		15	96	200
10	Monday, May 31, 2004	16	24		35
11	Friday, July 30, 2004		7	44	70
12	Friday, October 1, 2004	25	32	50	75
13	Sunday, October 10, 2004	4	5	6	10
14	Saturday, March 19, 2005	35	50		100
15	Thursday, April 28, 2005		2		0
16	Friday, May 27, 2005	20	25	83	100
17	Monday, May 30, 2005	5	6	19	30
18	Thursday, February 9, 2006		41		50
19	Friday, February 10, 2006	37	41	90	91

20	Thursday, March 2, 2006	4	5	54	50
21	Wednesday, April 12, 2006	47	58		100
22	Friday, June 2, 2006	6	7	7	8
23	Monday, June 26, 2006		8		26
24	Sunday, August 6, 2006		1		
25	Wednesday, November 8, 2006	40	43	25	39
26	Friday, November 17, 2006		1		2
27	Sunday, December 3, 2006		2		1
28	Monday, January 22, 2007		1		2
29	Monday, January 22, 2007		5	23	25
30	Friday, January 26, 2007		2	5	7
31	Saturday, January 27, 2007	12	14	30	60
32	Monday, January 29, 2007		3		7
33	Saturday, February 3, 2007		1		0
34	Saturday, February 3, 2007		3		8
35	Tuesday, February 6, 2007		1		3
36	Saturday, February 17, 2007		17		35
37	Thursday, March 29, 2007		3		7
38	Saturday, April 28, 2007	25	35	40	60
39	Tuesday, May 15, 2007	22	26	11	30
40	Monday, May 28, 2007		3		1
41	Wednesday, July 4, 2007	8	10		12
42	Thursday, July 12, 2007		5		3
43	Thursday, July 12, 2007		6		0
44	Saturday, July 14, 2007		24	26	28
45	Sunday, July 15, 2007		28		56
46	Sunday, July 15, 2007	21	22	40	45
47	Tuesday, July 17, 2007	16	17	50	70
48	Tuesday, July 17, 2007		5		3
49	Thursday, July 19, 2007		30		50
50	Thursday, July 19, 2007	7	8	30	35
51	Thursday, July 19, 2007	15	20		27
52	Friday, July 20, 2007		5		6

53	Friday, July 27, 2007	14	15	65	70
54	Friday, August 3, 2007		3		6
55	Saturday, August 4, 2007		9	35	43
56	Friday, August 17, 2007		1	3	5
57	Saturday, August 18, 2007		1		4
58	Saturday, August 18, 2007		3		1
59	Sunday, August 19, 2007		3		2
60	Monday, August 20, 2007	4	8	14	16
61	Friday, August 24, 2007		6	20	30
62	Friday, August 24, 2007		4		2
63	Sunday, August 26, 2007		5		2
64	Saturday, September 1, 2007		1		6
65	Saturday, September 1, 2007	6	7	4	11
66	Tuesday, September 4, 2007		18		50
67	Tuesday, September 4, 2007		7		20
68	Tuesday, September 11, 2007	17	20	16	19
69	Thursday, September 13, 2007	15	20	18	46
70	Saturday, September 22, 2007		1	1	3
71	Monday, October 1, 2007		16	29	32
72	Thursday, October 18, 2007	125	135	100	100
73	Thursday, October 25, 2007	20	30	34	35
74	Tuesday, October 30, 2007	7	9	28	31
75	Thursday, November 1, 2007	8	12	28	40
76	Friday, November 9, 2007	3	5	2	5
77	Saturday, November 24, 2007		36		35
78	Saturday, November 24, 2007		2		5
79	Tuesday, December 4, 2007		1		
80	Sunday, December 9, 2007	10	13		2
81	Monday, December 10, 2007		1	8	22
82	Thursday, December 13, 2007	7	14	22	23
83	Saturday, December 15, 2007	6	7	15	20
84	Monday, December 17, 2007		13	2	5
85	Friday, December 21, 2007		61		200

86	Sunday, December 23, 2007		10		23
87	Thursday, December 27, 2007	21	31	61	70
88	Monday, January 7, 2008		1	8	13
89	Thursday, January 10, 2008	24	27	73	80
90	Tuesday, January 15, 2008		1		
91	Thursday, January 17, 2008	10	13	25	25
92	Wednesday, January 23, 2008		2		1
93	Friday, February 1, 2008	5	8	13	15
94	Monday, February 4, 2008	8	11	45	47
95	Tuesday, February 5, 2008		1		2
96	Saturday, February 9, 2008	25	28	35	50
97	Monday, February 11, 2008	8	12		13
98	Saturday, February 16, 2008		3		14
99	Saturday, February 16, 2008	38	41	109	110
100	Monday, February 25, 2008	7	9	25	30
101	Friday, February 29, 2008	38	46	50	100
102	Saturday, March 1, 2008		3		23
103	Sunday, March 2, 2008	42	44	58	60
104	Tuesday, March 4, 2008	4	7	16	21
105	Tuesday, March 11, 2008	23	32		200
106	Tuesday, March 11, 2008	3	6		12
107	Monday, March 17, 2008	2	4	5	6
108	Thursday, March 20, 2008		6	9	11
109	Thursday, May 1, 2008		3	17	18
110	Tuesday, May 6, 2008	3	6	12	15
111	Friday, May 9, 2008		1	3	4
112	Sunday, May 18, 2008	12	14	24	25
113	Monday, June 2, 2008		9	25	30
114	Sunday, July 6, 2008	15	20	40	47
115	Sunday, July 13, 2008		1	3	4
116	Wednesday, August 13, 2008	8	10		20
117	Tuesday, August 19, 2008	30	33	40	45
118	Thursday, August 21, 2008	70	100	67	200

119	Friday, August 22, 2008		4		15
120	Saturday, August 23, 2008	7	16		20
121	Friday, August 29, 2008	3	7	29	37
122	Saturday, September 6, 2008		31	79	90
123	Tuesday, September 16, 2008	3	11	9	25
124	Thursday, September 18, 2008		2		0
125	Saturday, September 20, 2008	42	61	250	300
126	Saturday, September 20, 2008	6	13	5	20
127	Monday, September 22, 2008	9	13	3	10
128	Wednesday, September 24, 2008		2	23	25
129	Friday, September 26, 2008		5		0
130	Thursday, October 2, 2008	4	5		18
131	Monday, October 6, 2008	22	27	62	100
132	Thursday, October 9, 2008		1	8	12
133	Thursday, October 9, 2008		1		
134	Friday, October 10, 2008	51	86	100	200
135	Thursday, October 16, 2008		5		27
136	Sunday, October 26, 2008	10	12		5
137	Wednesday, October 29, 2008		1		14
138	Friday, October 31, 2008	9	11	24	25
139	Sunday, November 2, 2008		9		
140	Tuesday, November 4, 2008		8		4
141	Thursday, November 6, 2008	16	23	40	45
142	Thursday, November 6, 2008		3		
143	Tuesday, November 11, 2008	3	5	13	15
144	Wednesday, November 12, 2008		8	10	12
145	Monday, November 17, 2008		11		8
146	Thursday, November 20, 2008		10		
147	Friday, November 28, 2008		8		16
148	Monday, December 1, 2008		11		50
149	Wednesday, December 3, 2008		7	8	10
150	Friday, December 5, 2008	6	11	8	15
151	Tuesday, December 9, 2008		2		4

152	Sunday, December 28, 2008	36	38	16	28
153	Sunday, January 4, 2009		1		2
154	Sunday, January 4, 2009	7	11	21	25
155	Friday, January 23, 2009	2	3	12	25
156	Thursday, February 5, 2009		1		12
157	Thursday, February 5, 2009	30	33		55
158	Friday, February 6, 2009		1		7
159	Monday, February 9, 2009		6	17	18
160	Friday, February 20, 2009	32	33	150	200
161	Saturday, February 21, 2009		2		
162	Monday, February 23, 2009		2		2
163	Monday, March 2, 2009	5	7	11	12
164	Wednesday, March 11, 2009	4	5	3	6
165	Monday, March 16, 2009	14	16	17	25
166	Monday, March 23, 2009				2
167	Thursday, March 26, 2009	15	16		25
168	Friday, March 27, 2009	70	77	160	175
169	Monday, March 30, 2009		5		9
170	Thursday, April 2, 2009		1		0
171	Saturday, April 4, 2009	8	9	4	5
172	Saturday, April 4, 2009	5	9	10	39
173	Sunday, April 5, 2009	26	28	50	60
174	Wednesday, April 15, 2009	16	19	6	10
175	Saturday, April 18, 2009	21	28	61	65
176	Tuesday, May 5, 2009	7	12	25	48
177	Monday, May 11, 2009	10	12	19	20
178	Thursday, May 21, 2009	6	10	25	29
179	Wednesday, May 27, 2009	26	29	300	350
180	Thursday, May 28, 2009		6		4
181	Thursday, May 28, 2009		6	8	12
182	Friday, June 5, 2009		41	60	70
183	Saturday, June 6, 2009		3	4	5
184	Tuesday, June 9, 2009	11	16	60	80

185	Wednesday, June 10, 2009	1	3	13	15
186	Friday, June 12, 2009	6	8	5	8
187	Friday, June 12, 2009	4	8	90	103
188	Monday, June 22, 2009		3		7
189	Friday, June 26, 2009		3	3	4
190	Tuesday, June 30, 2009	7	9	8	10
191	Tuesday, June 30, 2009		5		11
192	Wednesday, July 1, 2009		1		0
193	Thursday, July 2, 2009		2	33	40
194	Wednesday, July 8, 2009		1		5
195	Tuesday, July 28, 2009		3	3	5
196	Thursday, August 13, 2009	4	7		3
197	Sunday, August 16, 2009	4	6		4
198	Saturday, August 15, 2009		2		3
199	Tuesday, August 18, 2009	1	4	3	8
200	Saturday, August 22, 2009		4	2	3
201	Thursday, August 27, 2009	21	23	5	27
202	Sunday, August 30, 2009	17	19	11	14
203	Saturday, September 12, 2009		1	2	4
204	Sunday, September 13, 2009		1	3	5
205	Sunday, September 13, 2009		1		
206	Friday, September 18, 2009	36	38	50	60
207	Saturday, September 19, 2009		3		1
208	Monday, September 21, 2009		1		0
209	Saturday, September 26, 2009	10	15	70	120
210	Saturday, September 26, 2009	10	11	50	65
211	Monday, September 28, 2009	4	6		
212	Monday, October 5, 2009		6	7	8
213	Friday, October 9, 2009	48	51	150	187
214	Monday, October 12, 2009		42	45	50
215	Thursday, October 15, 2009		12	20	22
216	Thursday, October 15, 2009		3		
217	Friday, October 16, 2009	14	16	19	21

218	Tuesday, October 20, 2009	6	7	29	40
219	Friday, October 23, 2009	9	10	15	17
220	Saturday, October 24, 2009		2		
221	Monday, November 2, 2009	36	39	60	63
222	Monday, November 2, 2009		3	20	25
223	Sunday, November 8, 2009	16	20	44	45
224	Monday, November 9, 2009	3	6	5	7
225	Tuesday, November 10, 2009	32	35	70	100
226	Friday, November 13, 2009	12	14	80	160
227	Friday, November 13, 2009		9	27	29
228	Saturday, November 14, 2009		13	25	35
229	Monday, November 16, 2009		4		43
230	Thursday, November 19, 2009	20	23	48	50
231	Tuesday, December 1, 2009	1	3	18	30
232	Wednesday, December 2, 2009		3	11	18
233	Friday, December 4, 2009	37	42	80	82
234	Monday, December 7, 2009	40	46	100	135
235	Monday, December 7, 2009	9	12	37	50
236	Tuesday, December 8, 2009	13	16	47	61
237	Tuesday, December 15, 2009	32	34	60	70
238	Thursday, December 17, 2009		1		
239	Friday, December 18, 2009		14	28	35
240	Tuesday, December 22, 2009		4	22	23
241	Thursday, December 24, 2009	4	6	24	25
242	Thursday, December 24, 2009		2		1
243	Monday, December 28, 2009	10	16	81	100
244	Monday, December 28, 2009		31		60
245	Friday, January 1, 2010	91	101	42	100
246	Tuesday, January 5, 2010		5	11	12
247	Friday, January 8, 2010		9		11
248	Friday, January 8, 2010		1		4
249	Saturday, January 16, 2010		2		2
250	Saturday, January 23, 2010	4	6	8	11

251	Saturday, January 30, 2010	16	18	44	47
252	Wednesday, February 10, 2010	17	19	8	11
253	Thursday, February 11, 2010		17	25	30
254	Thursday, February 18, 2010	30	32	80	101
255	Saturday, February 20, 2010		2	4	10
256	Monday, February 22, 2010	12	14	37	41
257	Saturday, February 27, 2010		5		23
258	Friday, March 5, 2010	12	15	33	35
259	Monday, March 8, 2010	13	15	80	100
260	Thursday, March 11, 2010		5		20
261	Friday, March 12, 2010	43	58	90	100
262	Saturday, March 13, 2010	14	18	52	60
263	Monday, March 29, 2010		3	5	8
264	Monday, March 29, 2010		3		2
265	Monday, April 5, 2010	10	11		20
266	Monday, April 5, 2010	50	53	80	100
267	Friday, April 16, 2010		12	35	40
268	Saturday, April 17, 2010	41	46	64	70
269	Sunday, April 18, 2010		8	31	32
270	Monday, April 19, 2010	23	25	42	49
271	Wednesday, April 28, 2010	4	6	12	14
272	Saturday, May 1, 2010		4	13	16
273	Friday, May 28, 2010	80	91	92	200
274	Thursday, July 1, 2010	40	45		175
275	Friday, July 9, 2010	65	82	104	110
276	Monday, July 12, 2010		1		0
277	Sunday, July 18, 2010		1	9	15
278	Monday, July 26, 2010		9	23	25
279	Wednesday, August 4, 2010	3	5	11	14
280	Monday, August 23, 2010	26	31		40
281	Wednesday, September 1, 2010	29	34	200	243
282	Friday, September 3, 2010		1		4
283	Friday, September 3, 2010	55	63	152	200

284	Monday, September 6, 2010	15	20	53	57
285	Thursday, September 9, 2010	4	6	4	6
286	Thursday, October 7, 2010	9	12	65	77
287	Monday, October 18, 2010		1	5	14
288	Monday, November 1, 2010	2	5	3	12
289	Friday, November 5, 2010	74	96	70	100
290	Thursday, November 11, 2010	18	21	120	140
291	Thursday, November 11, 2010		1		2
292	Sunday, November 14, 2010		2		8
293	Tuesday, November 30, 2010		7	22	25
294	Monday, December 6, 2010	42	52	75	100
295	Tuesday, December 7, 2010		1	10	12
296	Wednesday, December 8, 2010	19	21		32
297	Friday, December 10, 2010	15	18	22	30
298	Thursday, December 23, 2010		5		24
299	Thursday, December 23, 2010		2		2
300	Saturday, December 25, 2010	47	48	100	105
301	Monday, December 27, 2010		8		65
302	Wednesday, January 12, 2011		21	15	17
303	Tuesday, January 25, 2011	11	14	77	80
304	Tuesday, January 25, 2011		5		15
305	Thursday, January 27, 2011		0		0
306	Monday, January 31, 2011		7		19
307	Thursday, February 10, 2011	33	37	42	50
308	Saturday, February 12, 2011		2	1	3
309	Friday, February 18, 2011		1		4
310	Thursday, March 3, 2011	5	10	30	36
311	Wednesday, March 9, 2011	37	44		52
312	Thursday, March 24, 2011	5	9	25	30
313	Wednesday, March 30, 2011		11	21	23
314	Thursday, March 31, 2011		13	32	42
315	Friday, April 1, 2011		2	2	8
316	Sunday, April 3, 2011	44	48		100

317	Monday, April 4, 2011	8	10	26	30
318	Thursday, April 7, 2011		2	17	18
319	Saturday, April 23, 2011		6	5	8
320	Friday, May 13, 2011	82	97	140	150
321	Saturday, May 14, 2011		4		9
322	Wednesday, May 25, 2011	8	12	46	48
323	Thursday, May 26, 2011	29	33	56	60
324	Saturday, May 28, 2011		9		11
325	Sunday, June 5, 2011	18	20	28	45
326	Sunday, June 12, 2011		35		107
327	Monday, June 13, 2011	1	3	4	6
328	Saturday, June 25, 2011		12	3	5
329	Monday, July 11, 2011		8	25	26
330	Thursday, July 21, 2011		1		2
331	Sunday, July 24, 2011		2		7
332	Saturday, August 6, 2011		2		0
333	Thursday, August 11, 2011		8		17
334	Friday, August 19, 2011		57		123
335	Wednesday, August 31, 2011		12		22
336	Thursday, September 1, 2011		12		35
337	Wednesday, September 7, 2011	26	30	60	82
338	Thursday, September 15, 2011		46		63
339	Monday, September 19, 2011		9		30
340	Friday, October 28, 2011		3		2
341	Monday, November 7, 2011		4		9
342	Wednesday, November 16, 2011		7		0
343	Friday, November 18, 2011		1		
344	Saturday, December 24, 2011		6		12
345	Friday, December 30, 2011		16		33
346	Tuesday, January 3, 2012		2		
347	Saturday, January 14, 2012	7	8	7	10
348	Thursday, January 19, 2012		1		6
349	Monday, January 30, 2012	3	5	7	8

350	Thursday, February 16, 2012		2		3
351	Friday, February 17, 2012	26	29		36
352	Friday, February 24, 2012		7		6
353	Friday, March 2, 2012		26		20
354	Saturday, March 3, 2012		2	6	8
355	Sunday, March 4, 2012		1		3
356	Sunday, March 11, 2012	14	16	30	33
357	Thursday, March 15, 2012		2	2	5
358	Friday, March 23, 2012	7	14	9	10
359	Thursday, April 5, 2012		5		17
360	Friday, May 4, 2012	25	30	72	75
361	Friday, June 8, 2012		22		40
362	Tuesday, June 12, 2012	2	4		5
363	Monday, June 18, 2012		7		30
364	Thursday, June 28, 2012	13	15	24	30
365	Monday, July 16, 2012		1	2	5
366	Saturday, July 21, 2012		10		13
367	Thursday, August 16, 2012		11		3
368	Saturday, August 18, 2012		5		
369	Monday, September 3, 2012		3	20	21
370	Monday, September 10, 2012	14	16	40	80
371	Saturday, October 13, 2012	17	19	40	41
372	Saturday, November 3, 2012	5	7	7	10
373	Wednesday, November 7, 2012	6	9	36	37
374	Thursday, November 8, 2012		4	21	23
375	Monday, November 19, 2012		1	3	4
376	Wednesday, November 21, 2012	17	21	36	40
377	Sunday, November 25, 2012	5	7	70	80
378	Thursday, November 29, 2012		9	15	18
379	Tuesday, December 4, 2012		1	6	10
380	Tuesday, December 4, 2012		5	20	25
381	Monday, December 10, 2012		9		5
382	Saturday, December 22, 2012		8		17

383	Thursday, January 10, 2013		31		70
384	Thursday, January 10, 2013		106		169
385	Friday, February 1, 2013		27		40
386	Saturday, February 2, 2013		37		11
387	Friday, February 8, 2013		1		6
388	Thursday, February 14, 2013		11		23
389	Thursday, February 14, 2013		6		0
390	Friday, February 15, 2013		21		11
391	Saturday, February 16, 2013		85		200
392	Monday, February 18, 2013		8		5
393	Thursday, February 21, 2013				11
394	Thursday, March 14, 2013		9		10
395	Monday, March 18, 2013		5		29
396	Tuesday, March 19, 2013		48		0
397	Saturday, March 23, 2013		18		10
398	Friday, March 29, 2013		13		28
399	Saturday, March 30, 2013		2		7
400	Sunday, March 31, 2013		2		7
401	Sunday, March 31, 2013		2		2
402	Tuesday, April 9, 2013		18		3
403	Saturday, April 13, 2013		9		10
404	Sunday, April 14, 2013	3	6		0
405	Tuesday, April 16, 2013		9		8
406	Tuesday, April 16, 2013		9		49
407	Thursday, April 18, 2013		2		25
408	Saturday, April 20, 2013		5		4
409	Tuesday, April 23, 2013		7		40
410	Wednesday, April 24, 2013		1		2
411	Friday, April 26, 2013		11		0
412	Friday, April 26, 2013		0		6
413	Saturday, April 27, 2013		3		43
414	Monday, April 29, 2013		10		29
415	Wednesday, May 8, 2013		3		27

416	Wednesday, May 8, 2013		2		0
417	Sunday, May 12, 2013		6		58
418	Thursday, May 16, 2013		13		30
419	Saturday, May 18, 2013		35		52
420	Monday, May 20, 2013		2		4
421	Thursday, May 23, 2013		2		0
422	Friday, May 24, 2013		0		2
423	Monday, May 27, 2013		3		14
424	Wednesday, June 5, 2013		5		15
425	Wednesday, June 5, 2013		2		2
426	Saturday, June 15, 2013		15		
427	Saturday, June 15, 2013		12		
428	Friday, June 21, 2013		16		30
429	Wednesday, June 26, 2013		2		2
430	Sunday, June 30, 2013		29		60
431	Monday, July 1, 2013		29		70
432	Thursday, July 4, 2013		5		
433	Friday, July 5, 2013		7		19
434	Monday, July 8, 2013		9		11
435	Thursday, July 11, 2013		8		10
436	Wednesday, July 24, 2013		9		
437	Friday, July 26, 2013		59		206
438	Thursday, August 8, 2013		31		62
439	Tuesday, August 27, 2013		6		9
440	Sunday, September 8, 2013		4		12
441	Sunday, September 22, 2013		83		120
442	Wednesday, October 2, 2013		15		0
443	Wednesday, October 2, 2013		7		13
444	Thursday, October 3, 2013		14		10
445	Thursday, October 3, 2013		13		10
446	Friday, October 11, 2013		3		2
447	Wednesday, October 16, 2013		9		30
448	Saturday, November 16, 2013		7		4

449	Monday, November 18, 2013		7		
450	Friday, November 22, 2013		7		28
451	Monday, December 2, 2013		1		1
452	Tuesday, December 17, 2013		4		0
453	Wednesday, December 18, 2013		4		15
454	Friday, December 20, 2013		1		20
455	Wednesday, January 1, 2014		2		34
456	Monday, January 6, 2014		2		0
457	Thursday, January 9, 2014		4		10
458	Sunday, January 19, 2014		20		30
459	Monday, January 20, 2014		15		34
460	Thursday, January 23, 2014		6		8
461	Wednesday, January 29, 2014		4		2
462	Tuesday, February 4, 2014		10		50
463	Friday, February 7, 2014		1		5
464	Monday, February 10, 2014		5		5
465	Thursday, February 13, 2014		14		58
466	Friday, February 14, 2014		1		4
467	Monday, February 24, 2014		5		12
468	Monday, March 3, 2014		13		29
469	Friday, March 14, 2014		10		25
470	Thursday, April 24, 2014		5		3
471	Sunday, May 11, 2014		5		9
472	Wednesday, June 4, 2014		6		
473	Monday, June 9, 2014		28		24
474	Monday, June 9, 2014		5		0
475	Tuesday, June 24, 2014		7		
476	Tuesday, September 23, 2014		5		14
477	Saturday, October 4, 2014		6		20
478	Wednesday, October 15, 2014		8		17
479	Thursday, October 23, 2014		3		30
480	Sunday, November 2, 2014	55	62	100	129
481	Tuesday, December 16, 2014		148		132

482	Sunday, December 28, 2014		2		0
483	Friday, January 30, 2015	60	62		39
484	Friday, February 13, 2015		21		60
485	Tuesday, February 17, 2015	5	9		
486	Wednesday, February 18, 2015		5		6
487	Sunday, March 15, 2015		17	70	72
488	Friday, March 20, 2015		3		

Location					
No	**Place**	**City**	**Province**	**Address**	**Geolocation**
1	Egyptian Embassy	Islamabad	Punjab	Embassy of Egypt	33° 43' 10.71" N, 73° 6' 20.30" E
2	Office of the Nawa-e-Waqt group	Karachi	Sindh	Nawa-e-Waqt Karachi	
3	In A Navy Bus	Karachi	Sindh	Near Sheraton Hotel Club Road	24° 50' 55.31" N,67° 1' 43.16" E
4	US Consulate	Karachi	Sindh	US Consulate, Mai Kolachi Bypass	24° 50' 28.29" N,67° 0' 34.55" E
5	Imambargah	Quetta	Balochistan	Mekangi Road gate Imambargah	30° 10' 58.70" N,66° 59' 55.44" E
6	Chaklala bridge	Rawalpindi	Punjab	Chaklala bridge	33° 36' 19.34" N,73° 3' 50.82" E
7	Jhanda Chichi	Rawalpindi	Punjab	Jhanda Chichi	33° 35' 27.09" N,73° 4' 28.09" E

8	Imambargah	Rawalpindi	Punjab	Imambargah Yadgar-e-Hussain(as) Satellite town	33° 38' 21.69'' N,73° 4' 3.68'' E
9	Sindh Madressatul Islam	Karachi	Sindh	Sindh Madresatul Islam University, Aiwan-e-Tijarat Road	24° 51' 2.63'' N,67° 0' 14.51'' E
10	Imambargah	Karachi	Sindh	Masjid O Imambargah Ali Raza, Zainabia Road	24° 52' 11.96'' N,67° 2' 1.51'' E
11	Fateh Jang	Attock	Punjab	Jaffar Village	33° 34' 2.21'' N,72° 38' 26.61'' E
12	Imambargah	Sialkot	Punjab	Raja Road	32° 29' 32.92'' N,74° 31' 51.74'' E
13	Imambargah	Lahore	Punjab	Jamia Masjid Kashmirian in Mochi Gate	31° 34' 38.73'' N,74° 19' 18.11'' E
14	At a Shrine	Jhal Magsi	Balochistan	Fatehpur Village	28° 25' 2.67'' N,67° 34' 15.07'' E
15	Biadara	Swat	KPK	Biadara Village	33° 31' 48.00'' N,71° 3' 36.00'' E
16	Bari Imam Shrine	Islamabad	Punjab	Islamabad	33° 43' 44.32'' N,73° 7' 12.75'' E
17	Imambargah	Karachi	Sindh	Gulshan e Iqbal	24° 55' 9.24'' N,67° 5' 40.51'' E

18	Hangu Town	Hango	KPK	Hango Town	33° 31' 48.00" N,71° 3' 36.00" E
19	Hangu Tall Road	Hango	KPK	Main Hango-Tall road	33° 31' 48.00" N,71° 3' 36.00" E
20	US Consulate	Karachi	Sindh	Near Marriot Hotel	24° 50' 28.29" N,67° 0' 34.55" E
21	Nishtar Park	Karachi	Sindh	Nishtar Park Road	24° 52' 29.48" N,67° 2' 2.77" E
22	Baka Khel	Bannu	KPK	Bannu Mirali Road	32° 57' 0.00" N,70° 30' 0.00" E
23	Checkpoint	Miramshah	N/A	Miramshah Bannu Road	33° 0' 0.00" N,70° 3' 54.00" E
24	Near Zehri Street	Hub	Balochistan	Main Market	25° 3' 10.44" N,66° 54' 46.48" E
25	Punjab Regiment Centre	Malakand	KPK	Punjab Regiment Centre Dargai	34° 30' 10.95" N,71° 54' 16.43" E
26	Ring Road	Peshawar	KPK	Fayaz Khalil Shaheed Chowk	33° 58' 36.70" N,71° 33' 5.59" E
27	Near Speen Tangi	Bannu	KPK	Kohat bannu Road	29° 56' 39.27" N,68° 5' 48.97" E
28	Mirali	North Waziristan	N/A	N/A	N/A
29	Khajori Checkpost	Miramshah	N/A	Khajori, Miran Shah Bannu Road	32° 56' 51.09" N,70° 19' 28.33" E
30	Marriott Hotel	Islamabad	Punjab	Marriott Hotel	33° 43' 45.80" N,73° 5' 35.33" E

31	Qissakhwani Bazaar	Peshawar	KPK	Qissa Khawani Bazar Andar Shehr	34° 0' 28.34" N,71° 34' 13.74" E
32	Checkpoint Near Liaquat Park	Dera Ismail Khan	KPK	Liaquat Park ECircular Road	31° 49' 46.39" N,70° 54' 41.36" E
33	Ghaznikhel Market	Lakki Marwat	KPK	Ghazni Khel	32° 33' 35.25" N,70° 44' 31.64" E
34	Bara Khel	Tank	FATA	Bara Khel	32° 8' 59.07" N,70° 26' 3.35" E
35	Islamabad Airport	Islamabad	Punjab	Benazir Bhutto International Airport	33° 36' 28.41" N,73° 6' 1.46" E
36	Court Room	Quetta	Balochistan	Quetta Kacheri	30° 11' 53.65" N,67° 0' 39.25" E
37	Guliana Training Centre	Kharian	Punjab	Kharian	32° 48' 51.34" N,73° 52' 59.05" E
38	Charsadda	Peshawar	KPK	Charsadda	34° 12' 59.24" N,71° 42' 53.26" E
39	Marhaba Restaurant	peshawar	KPK	N/A	N/A
40	Boltonabad			Naz	N/A
41	Near Khajori Checkpost	Bannu	KPK	Near Darul Uloom Sadiqia	32° 59' 38.88" N,70° 35' 52.11" E
42	Outside Political AgentOffice	Miramshah	N\A	Miramshah	33° 0' 0.00" N,70° 3' 54.00" E
43	Mosque	Swat	KPK	Swat	35° 13' 21.76" N,72° 25' 32.93" E

44	Daznaray	Miramshah	N\A	North Waziristan Agency	32° 58' 28.70" N,70° 8' 44.09" E
45	Police Recruitment Centre	Dera Ismail Khan	KPK	Police Line	31° 49' 0.00" N,70° 55' 0.00" E
46	Matta	Swat	KPK	Matta	34° 55' 50.54" N,72° 25' 0.98" E
47	F8 Islamabad	Islamabad	Punjab	F8 Islamabad	33° 41' 59.74" N,73° 2' 45.54" E
48	Khajori Checkpost	Miramshah	FATA	Khajori Checkpost	33° 0' 0.00" N,70° 3' 54.00" E
49	RCD Highway	Hub	Balochistan	RCD Highway	25° 1' 32.47" N,66° 53' 12.71" E
50	Police Training College	Hangu	KPK	Police Training Centre	33° 32' 13.42" N,71° 4' 12.32" E
51	Army mosque	Kohat	KPK	Pathan Line Center	33° 35' 23.38" N,71° 26' 53.04" E
52	Tochi scouts Checkpost	Miramshah	N\A	Tochi Scouts checkpost	33° 0' 0.00" N,70° 3' 54.00" E
53	Muzaffargarh Hotel	Islamabad	N\A	Aabpara Market	33° 43' 45.80" N,73° 5' 35.33" E
54	Matta	Swat	KPK	Gora village	34° 55' 50.54" N,72° 25' 0.98" E
55	Taxi Stand	Parachinar	N\A	Taxi stand	33° 53' 57.00" N,70° 6' 3.00" E
56	Manzai	Tank	N\A	Manzai	32° 15' 5.37" N,70° 14' 43.07" E

57	Bannu	Bannu	KPK	Bannu	32° 59' 10.00" N,70° 36' 15.00" E
58	Miramshah Checkpost	Miramshah	N\A	Miramshah Checkpost	32° 59' 10.00" N,70° 36' 15.00" E
59	Mirali	North Waziristan	N\A	Army Checkpost	32° 58' 14.53" N,70° 16' 40.93" E
60	Mandori Village	Thall	KPK	Mandori Checkpost	33° 27' 39.77" N,70° 25' 45.87" E
61	Qamar Checkpost	Mirali	N\A	Qamar Checkpost	32° 58' 14.53" N,70° 16' 40.93" E
62	Asad Khel	Asad Khel	N\A	Asad Khel	32° 50' 7.23" N,70° 3' 49.36" E
63	Shangla	Shagla	KPK	Shangla District, KPK	34° 45' 50.09" N,72° 21' 54.54" E
64	Jandola Area	Jandola Area	FATA	Jandola SWA	
65	Mamond Tehsil	Bajaur	N\A	Mamond Tehsil	34° 51' 24.85" N,71° 25' 47.77" E
66	Qasim Market	Rawalpindi	Punjab	Qasim Market	33° 36' 4.31" N,73° 2' 4.05" E
67	R A Bazar	Rawalpindi	Punjab	R A Bazar	33° 35' 14.36" N,73° 2' 21.27" E
68	Bannu Adda	Dera Ismail Khan	KPK	Dera Ismail Khan	31° 49' 0.00" N,70° 55' 0.00" E
69	Army Mess	Haripur	Punjab	Tarbela Ghazi	33° 58' 53.14" N,72° 36' 33.48" E

70	Customs Checkpost	Tank	KPK	Customs Checkpoint	32° 12' 51.47" N,70° 22' 39.83" E
71	Checkpoint	Bannu	kPK	Checkpoint	32° 59' 10.00" N,70° 36' 15.00" E
72	Karsaz	Karachi	Sindh	Karsaz	24° 53' 20.59" N,67° 6' 0.28" E
73	Police Line	Swat	KPK	Mingora	34° 46' 25.13" N,72° 21' 35.64" E
74	President Camp Office	Rawalpindi	Punjab	Golf Road	33° 34' 47.50" N,73° 4' 26.41" E
75	Sargodha Faisalabad Road 49 Tale	Sargodha	Punjab	Sargodha Faisalabad Road	31° 49' 3.28" N,72° 49' 25.19" E
76	Hayatabad	Peshawar	KPK	Hayatabad	33° 59' 10.00" N,71° 27' 25.00" E
77	Hamza Camp	Rawalpindi	Punjab	.Hamza Camp Faizabad	33° 39' 48.63" N,73° 5' 2.62" E
78	Checkpoint General Headquarters	Rawalpindi	Punjab	Checkpoint General Headquaeters	33° 35' 54.22" N,73° 2' 38.89" E
79	Checkpoint Cantonment Area	Peshawar	KPK	Cantonment Area Babar Road	34° 0' 37.94" N,71° 32' 40.23" E
80	Ningolai Checkpoint	Mingora	KPK	Ningolai Checkpoint	34° 46' 25.13" N,72° 21' 35.64" E
81	Military Base Kamra	Attock	Punjab	Pakisatan Aeronautical Complex Kamra	33° 47' 10.24" N,72° 21' 31.08" E

82	Kachmore Checkpoint	Quetta	Balochistan	Hanna Road Kachmore	30° 10' 58.70" N,66° 59' 55.44" E
83	Checkpost	Nowshera	KPK	Nowshera Cantonment	34° 0' 19.82" N,72° 0' 29.87" E
84	Kohat Cantonment	Kohat	KPK	Kohat Cantonment	33° 35' 9.63" N,71° 26' 39.60" E
85	Mosque	Charsadda	KPK	Markazi Jamia Masjid, Sherpao Village	34° 15' 49.04" N,71° 41' 54.54" E
86	Mingora	Sawat	KPK	Mingora	34° 46' 25.13" N,72° 21' 35.64" E
87	Liaqat Bagh	Rawalpindi	Punjab	Liaqat Bagh Rawalpindi	33° 35' 54.22" N,73° 2' 38.89" E
88	Frontier House	Swat	KPK	Frontier House Kabal	34° 47' 36.80" N,72° 17' 25.48" E
89	G.P.O Chowk	Lahore	Punjab	G.P.O Chowk Near Lahore High Court	31° 33' 50.57" N,74° 18' 52.62" E
90	Checkpoint	Mohmand Agency	N\A	Ghalanai Checkpoint	34° 19' 16.00" N,71° 24' 0.00" E
91	Imam Bargah	Peshawar	KPK	Imam Bargah Mohala Jangi Qisakhwani Bazar	34° 0' 53.91" N,71° 34' 49.76" E
92	Kharkhano	Peshawar	KPK	Near police checkpost at border of Khyber agency and Peshawer	

93	Kajhori Checkpoint	Mirali	N\A	Kajhori checkpoint Mirali North Waziristan	32° 19' 12.85" N,69° 51' 35.07" E
94	R.A Bazar	Rawalpindi	Punjab	R.A Bazar Rawalpindi	33° 35' 14.36" N,73° 2' 21.27" E
95	Sabzal Road	Quetta	Balochistan	Sabzal Road Quetta	30° 11' 35.49" N,66° 58' 53.43" E
96	Nakai, Charsadda	Peshawar	KPK	Shabqadar Charsadda	34° 8' 57.96" N,71° 44' 34.01" E
97	Aidak	North Waziristan	N\A	Aidak North Waziristan	32° 19' 12.85" N,69° 51' 35.07" E
98	Gulkada	Mingora	KPK	Gulkada Mingora	34° 45' 50.09" N,72° 21' 54.54" E
99	Parachinar	Kurram Agency	N\A	Parachinar Kurram Agency	33° 53' 57.00" N,70° 6' 3.00" E
100	Mall Road	Rawalpindi	Punjab	Mall Road Rawalpindi	33° 35' 14.36" N,73° 2' 21.27" E
101	Mingora	Peshawar	KPK	Mingora Peshawar	34° 46' 25.13" N,72° 21' 35.64" E
102	Khar	Bajaur Agency	N\A	Khar Bajuar Agency	34° 44' 24.00" N,71° 31' 48.00" E
103	Zarghoonkhel	Darra Adamkhel	N\A	Darra Adamkhel	33° 41' 40.03" N,71° 29' 45.07" E
104	Navy War Collage	Lahore	punjab	Navy War Collage Mall Road	31° 33' 19.09" N,74° 19' 56.85" E

105	F.I.A Headquarter	Lahore	Punjab	Regal Chowk	31° 26' 37.81" N,74° 17' 36.65" E
106	F Block Model Town	Lahore	Punjab	F Block Model Town	31° 28' 38.67" N,74° 19' 6.06" E
107	Police Line	Mingora	KPK	Police Line Mingora	34° 46' 25.13" N,72° 21' 35.64" E
108	Zarinoor	South Waziristan	N\A	Zarinoor South Waziristan	32° 18' 17.00" N,69° 34' 13.00" E
109	Mosque	Khyber Agency	N\A	Bara Khyber Agency	34° 1' 15.97" N,71° 17' 14.72" E
110	Checkpoint	Bannu	KPK	Bannu	32° 59' 10.00" N,70° 36' 15.00" E
111	Police station	Swat	KPK	Mingora	34° 46' 25.13" N,72° 21' 35.64" E
112	Bakery	Mardan	KPK	Mardan Cantt	34° 12' 0.72" N,72° 2' 27.99" E
113	Danish Embassy	Islamabad	Punjab	Street 18 Islamabad	33° 43' 45.80" N,73° 5' 35.33" E
114	Melody Chowk	Islamabad	Punjab	Sadar Road Melody Market	33° 43' 45.80" N,73° 5' 35.33" E
115	Kotli Imam Hussain	D.I Khan	KPK	Kotli Imam Hussain	31° 49' 0.00" N,70° 55' 0.00" E
116	Police station	Lahore	Punjab	Allama Iqbal Town	31° 30' 40.00" N,74° 17' 2.00" E
117	Hospital	D.I Khan	KPK	District Headquarter Hospital	31° 49' 0.00" N,70° 55' 0.00" E

118	Ordnance Factory	Wah Cantt	Punjab	Ordnance Factory Wah Cantt	33° 46' 7.79" N,72° 45' 55.96" E
119	Momin Town	Peshawar	KPK	Momin Town Peshawar	34° 1' 45.75" N,71° 36' 22.13" E
120	Police Station	Swat	KPK	Charbagh	34° 49' 60.00" N,72° 26' 30.00" E
121	Kohat Tunnel	Darra Adamkhel	N\A	Kohat Tunnel	33° 41' 40.03" N,71° 29' 45.07" E
122	Checkpoint	Peshawar	KPK	Zangli Checkpoint	34° 0' 53.91" N,71° 34' 49.76" E
123	Checkpoint	Swat	KPK	Kabal Checkpoint	35° 13' 21.76" N,72° 25' 32.93" E
124	Dir Upper Town	Dir Bala	KPK	Upper Dir Town, NWFP	
125	Marriott Hotel	Islamabad	Punjab	Marriott Hotel Islamabad	33° 43' 45.80" N,73° 5' 35.33" E
126	Norak	Miranshah	N\A	Norak Miranshah	33° 0' 0.00" N,70° 3' 54.00" E
127	Check post in Madyan, Swat	Swat	KPK	Madyan Swat	35° 7' 60.00" N,72° 31' 60.00" E
128	Near Askari Park	Quetta	Balochistan	Airport Road Quetta	30° 13' 19.74" N,67° 0' 19.62" E
129	A house in Karachi	Karachi	Sindh	A house in Karachi	
130	House of ANP Chied Asfandyar Wali	Charsadda	KPK	Wali Bagh Charsadda	34° 8' 57.96" N,71° 44' 34.01" E

131	Bhakkar	Lahore	Punjab	Bhakkar Punjab	31° 37' 22.80" N,71° 3' 45.36" E
132	Police Line	Islamabad	Punjab	Islamabad Police Line	33° 43' 45.80" N,73° 5' 35.33" E
133	Pak Afghan Road	Landi Kotal	N\A	Pak Afghan Road Landi Kotal	34° 5' 27.56" N,71° 8' 44.71" E
134	Khadezai	Orakzai Agency	N\A	Khadezai	33° 38' 28.74" N,70° 46' 57.84" E
135	Police station	Swat	KPK	Mingora Police Station Swat	34° 46' 13.76" N,72° 21' 33.57" E
136	Naqi Checkpost	Mohmand Agency	N\A	Naqi Checkpost	34° 33' 55.78" N,71° 28' 38.74" E
137	Checkpost	Bannu	KPK	Checkpost Near Combined Military Hospital	32° 55' 47.18" N,70° 40' 9.35" E
138	Police Chief Office	Mardan	KPK	D.I.G Police Office Mardan	34° 12' 0.41" N,72° 3' 2.88" E
139	Zaalai Checkpost	Wana	N\A	Zaalai Checkpost wana	32° 18' 17.00" N,69° 34' 13.00" E
140	Checkpost	Hangu	KPK	Hangu	33° 31' 48.00" N,71° 3' 36.00" E
141	Salarzai Tehsil	Bajaur	N\A	Salarzai Tehsil Bajaur	34° 51' 24.85" N,71° 25' 47.77" E
142	Police Line Checkpost	Swat	KPK	Police Line Checkpost	35° 13' 21.76" N,72° 25' 32.93" E

143	Qayum Stadium	Peshawar	KPK	Qayum Stadium Peshawar	34° 0' 53.91" N,71° 34' 49.76" E
144	Government High School	Peshawar	KPK	Government High School Shabqadar	34° 13' 20.32" N,71° 33' 21.88" E
145	Khawazakhela Checkpoint	Swat	KPK	Khawazakhela Checkpoint	34° 56' 13.42" N,72° 28' 7.37" E
146	Mosque	Bajaur	N\A	Bajaur Agency	34° 51' 24.85" N,71° 25' 47.77" E
147	Tarezi Bannu	Bannu	KPK	Tarezi Bannu District	
148	Sangota Checkpost	Mingora	KPK	Sangota Checkpost mingora Swat	34° 46' 25.13" N,72° 21' 35.64" E
149	Shabqadar	Peshawar	KPK	Shabqadar Charsadda	34° 8' 57.96" N,71° 44' 34.01" E
150	Kalaia	Orakzai Agency	N\A	Orakzai Agency	33° 41' 50.18" N,71° 8' 41.47" E
151	Nari Oba, Buner	Peshawar	KPK	Buner Peshawar	34° 0' 53.91" N,71° 34' 49.76" E
152	Shalbandi, Buner Polling Station	Peshawar	KPK	Government High School Shalbandi	34° 30' 29.64" N,72° 31' 14.62" E
153	Officers colony Bannu	Bannu	KPK	Officers Colony, Bannu	
154	Near Polytechnic College	Dera Ismail Khan	KPK	Polytechnic College D.I Khan	31° 49' 0.00" N,70° 55' 0.00" E
155	Checkpost	Swat	KPK	Swat	35° 13' 21.76" N,72° 25' 32.93" E

156	Police Station	Mingora	KPK	Mingora Town	
157	ImamBargah	Dera Ghazi Khan	Punjab	Johar Ali Imambargah Muslim Town	35° 13' 21.76" N,72° 25' 32.93" E
158	Teddi Bazar	Jamrud	N/A	Peshawar Torkham Highway	34° 0' 7.82" N,71° 22' 43.05" E
159	Checkpoint	Bannu	KPK	Baran Pul Bannu	32° 58' 37.24" N,70° 32' 3.01" E
160	Dera Bannu Road	Dera Ismail Khan	KPK	Dera Bannu Road D.I Khan	31° 49' 0.00" N,70° 55' 0.00" E
161	Lakki Town	Bannu	KPK	Lakki Town	32° 59' 10.00" N,70° 36' 15.00" E
162	Police Officer House	Bannu	KPK	Bannu	32° 59' 10.00" N,70° 36' 15.00" E
163	Madressa	Pishin	Balochistan	Killi Karbla Pishin	30° 35' 3.17" N,66° 59' 44.96" E
164	Namak Mandi	Peshawar	KPK	Namak Mandi Road	34° 0' 19.09" N,71° 33' 57.60" E
165	Pirwadhai	Rawalpindi	Punjab	Pirwadhai Rawalpindi	33° 37' 55.44" N,73° 2' 20.59" E
166	Special Branch Police Office	Islamabad	Punjab	Sitara Market Islamabad	33° 43' 45.80" N,73° 5' 35.33" E
167	Hotel	Tank	N/A	Jandola Tank	32° 19' 59.00" N,70° 6' 52.00" E
168	Mosque	Jamrud	N/A	Baghiari Checkpost Jamrud	34° 0' 0.00" N,71° 22' 60.00" E

169	Checkpost	Bannu	KPK	Mirzail Checkpost Bannu	32° 59' 10.00" N,70° 36' 15.00" E
170	Haryan Kot	Dargai	KPK	Haryan Kot, Dargai	
171	Checkpost	Islamabad	Punjab	F.C Checkpost Near Margalla Road	33° 43' 45.80" N,73° 5' 35.33" E
172	Checkpost	Miranshah	N/A	Civil Colony Checkpost	33° 0' 0.00" N,70° 3' 54.00" E
173	ImamBargah	Chakwal	Punjab	Mohala Sarpak	32° 55' 49.00" N,72° 51' 20.00" E
174	Checkpost	Charsadda	KPK	Hari Chand Checkpost tehsil Tangi	34° 10' 0.25" N,71° 45' 17.90" E
175	Checkpost	Hangu	KPK	Doaba Tehsil Hangu	33° 25' 25.00" N,70° 44' 11.00" E
176	Checkpost	Bara	KPK	Bara Qadeem Checkpost	33° 55' 0.99" N,71° 27' 47.58" E
177	Checkpost	Darra Adamkhel	N/A	F.C Checkpost Darra Adamkhel	33° 41' 40.03" N,71° 29' 45.07" E
178	F.C Fort	Jandola	N/A	F.C Fort Jandola	32° 19' 59.00" N,70° 6' 52.00" E
179	Rescue 15 Office	Lahore	Punjab	Rescue 15 Office Lahore	31° 33' 16.58" N,74° 21' 25.77" E
180	Checkpost	Peshawar	KPK	Mattni Kohat Road Peshawar	34° 0' 4.56" N,71° 33' 35.83" E

181	Checkpost	D.I Khan	KPK	Checkpost Near Rehmania Hospital	31° 49' 22.31" N,70° 53' 35.76" E
182	Mosque	Dir Bala	KPK	Hayagai Sharqai Village	34° 0' 53.91" N,71° 34' 49.76" E
183	Rescue 15 Office	Islamabad	Punjab	G 8/4 Sector	33° 41' 59.74" N,73° 2' 45.54" E
184	P.C Hotel	Peshawar	KPK	Khyber Road	34° 0' 53.91" N,71° 34' 49.76" E
185	Lateefabad's Ring Road	Peshawar	KPK	Ring Road	33° 58' 49.65" N,71° 26' 34.74" E
186	Madressa	Lahore	Punjab	Jamia Naeemia Road	31° 35' 18.98" N,74° 22' 1.74" E
187	Mosque	Nowshera	KPK	Nowshera Cantt	34° 0' 19.82" N,72° 0' 29.87" E
188	Thakot, Battagram	Battagram District	KPK	Thakot Police Checkpost	
189	Near Army Public School	Muzaffarabad	N/A	Near Army Public School	34° 21' 34.87" N,73° 28' 15.79" E
190	Pak Afghan Border	Landi Kotal	N/A	Pak Afgan Border Torkham	34° 5' 27.56" N,71° 8' 44.71" E
191	Hotel	Kalat	Balochistan	Quetta Karachi RCD Highway	29° 1' 33.00" N,66° 35' 23.00" E
192	Mashokhel, Mera, Peshawar	Peshawar	KPK	Mashokhel, Mera, Peshawer	
193	Chur Chowk	Rawalpindi	Punjab	Chur Chowk	33° 35' 54.22" N,73° 2' 38.89" E

194	Nasir Bagh Road	Peshawar	KPK	Nasir Bagh Road	34° 0' 31.30" N,71° 27' 41.43" E
195	Checkpost	Miranshah	N/A	Ghulam Khan Road	33° 0' 19.76" N,70° 3' 49.66" E
196	Wana Bazar	Wana	N/A	Wana Bazar	32° 18' 17.00" N,69° 34' 13.00" E
197	Checkpost	Swat	KPK	Charbagh Swat	34° 49' 60.00" N,72° 26' 30.00" E
198	Checkpost	Mingora	KPK	Checkpost Mingora	34° 46' 25.13" N,72° 21' 35.64" E
199	Bannu checkpost	Miranshah	N/A	Bannu Miranshah Road	33° 0' 0.00" N,70° 3' 54.00" E
200	Kabal	Swat	KPK	Kabal Swat	34° 47' 32.22" N,72° 16' 57.07" E
201	Checkpost	Landi Kotal	N/A	Torkham Border	34° 7' 20.49" N,71° 5' 37.55" E
202	Police Training Centre	Mingora	KPK	Police Training Centre	34° 46' 25.13" N,72° 21' 35.64" E
203	Police Station	Hangu	KPK	Doaba Police Station	33° 25' 34.05" N,70° 44' 25.62" E
204	Thana	Malakand	KPK	Malakand	34° 30' 10.95" N,71° 54' 16.43" E
205	Checkpost	Lower Dir	KPK	Maidan Checkpost	34° 50' 43.19" N,71° 54' 16.43" E
206	Kacha Pakha Bazar	Kohat	KPK	Kacha Pakha	33° 36' 6.76" N,71° 15' 55.65" E

207	Checkpost	Darra Adamkhel	N/A	Darra Adamkhel	33° 44' 3.78" N,71° 30' 53.15" E
208	Tatalai	Tatalai	KPK	Tatalai District	
209	Fakhr e Alam Road	Peshawar	KPK	Fakhr e Alam Road	34° 0' 1.66" N,71° 32' 33.87" E
210	Police Station	Bannu	KPK	Mandan Police Station	32° 59' 10.00" N,70° 36' 15.00" E
211	Baka Khel	Bannu	KPK	Baka Khel	32° 57' 0.00" N,70° 30' 0.00" E
212	World Food Program Office	Islamabad	Punjab	Sector F-8	33° 41' 59.74" N,73° 2' 45.54" E
213	Khyber Bazar	Peshawar	KPK	Khyber Bazar	34° 0' 33.74" N,71° 33' 56.19" E
214	Alpuri	Shangla	KPK	Alpuri Police Station	34° 54' 16.38" N,72° 38' 32.88" E
215	Police Station	Kohat	KPK	Police Station Kohat	33° 35' 0.24" N,71° 25' 59.59" E
216	Elliot Force Training Centre	Lahore	Punjab	Bedian Road	31° 27' 46.75" N,74° 26' 8.27" E
217	C.I.A Centre	Peshawar	KPK	C.I.A Centre Near Swati Gate	34° 0' 53.91" N,71° 34' 49.76" E
218	Islamic University	Islamabad	Punjab	Sector H 10	33° 43' 45.80" N,73° 5' 35.33" E
219	Pakistan Aeronautical Complex	Kamra	Punjab	Pakistan Aeronauticals Complex	33° 51' 20.89" N,72° 23' 39.89" E

220	Motorway Interchange	Lahore	Punjab	Kallar Kahar	32° 46' 33.72" N,72° 42' 3.06" E
221	Outside Bank	Rawalpindi	Punjab	National Bank Mall Road	33° 35' 54.22" N,73° 2' 38.89" E
222	Babu Sabu Interchange	Lahore	Punjab	Babu Sabu Interchange	32° 20' 25.14" N,73° 0' 28.65" E
223	Cattle Market	Peshawar	KPK	Ittefaq Chowk	33° 47' 32.71" N,71° 33' 44.56" E
224	Checkpost	Peshawar	KPK	Ring Road	33° 58' 49.65" N,71° 26' 34.74" E
225	Farooq e Azam Chowk	Charsadda	KPK	Farooq e Azam Chowk Tangi Road	34° 8' 57.96" N,71° 44' 34.01" E
226	Outside ISI Office	Peshawar	KPK	Khyber Road	34° 0' 53.91" N,71° 34' 49.76" E
227	Police Station	Bannu	KPK	Thana Baka Khel	32° 59' 10.00" N,70° 36' 15.00" E
228	Checkpost	Peshawar	KPK	Pishtakhara Ring Road	33° 58' 49.65" N,71° 26' 34.74" E
229	Checkpoint	Peshawar	KPK	Badaber Police Station	33° 54' 29.79" N,71° 33' 27.97" E
230	Kacheri Gate	Peshawar	KPK	District Court	34° 0' 53.91" N,71° 34' 49.76" E
231	Kabal	Swat	KPK	Kabal Swat	34° 47' 36.80" N,72° 17' 25.48" E
232	Naval Headquarters	Islamabad	Punjab	F-8 & E-8 Zafar Chowk	33° 43' 25.64" N,73° 0' 27.63" E

233	Mosque	Rawalpindi	Punjab	Parade Lane Rawalpindi Cantt	33° 35' 53.49" N,73° 2' 13.95" E
234	Market	Lahore	Punjab	Moon Market Allama Iqbal Town	31° 31' 13.89" N,74° 17' 30.61" E
235	Session Court Gate	Peshawar	KPK	Jail Road	34° 0' 53.91" N,71° 34' 49.76" E
236	Outside ISI Office	Multan	Punjab	Qasim Bela	30° 11' 39.24" N,71° 23' 44.61" E
237	Khosa Market	Dera Ghazi Khan	Punjab	Khosa Market	30° 3' 10.33" N,70° 38' 24.21" E
238	Essa Khel Village	Bannu	KPK	Essa Khel Village	32° 59' 10.00" N,70° 36' 15.00" E
239	Outside Mosque	Lower Dir	KPK	Police Line	34° 50' 43.19" N,71° 54' 16.43" E
240	Press Club	Peshawar	KPK	Press Club	34° 0' 53.91" N,71° 34' 49.76" E
241	Checkpoint	Peshawar	KPK	Near P.I.A Building	34° 0' 53.91" N,71° 34' 49.76" E
242	Outside Imambargah	Islamabad	Punjab	Shakrial Area	33° 38' 14.91" N,73° 6' 6.36" E
243	Outside Imambargah	Muzaffarabad	N/A	Imambargah	34° 21' 34.87" N,73° 28' 15.79" E
244	M.A Jinnah Road	Karachi	Sindh	M.A Jinnah Road	24° 51' 38.83" N,67° 1' 4.09" E
245	Playground	LakkiMarwat	KPK	Shah Hassan Khel	32° 25' 53.14" N,70° 57' 54.30" E

246	Army Barrack	Tarar Khel	N/A	Azad Jammu Kashmir	33° 55' 33.26" N,73° 46' 51.72" E
247	Tirah	Tira, Khyber Agency	FATA	Tirah Area	
248	Adezai	Peshawar	KPK	Adezai Village Mattani	
249	Rawalakot	Rawalakot	N/A	Azad Jammu Kashmir	33° 55' 33.26" N,73° 46' 51.72" E
250	Police Station	Tank	KPK	Gomal Police Station	32° 12' 51.47" N,70° 22' 39.83" E
251	Checkpoint	Bajaur Agency	N/A	Bajaur Agency	34° 51' 24.85" N,71° 25' 47.77" E
252	Jamrud	Khyber Agency	N/A	Jamrud Khyber Agency	34° 0' 0.00" N,71° 22' 60.00" E
253	Police Lines	Bannu	KPK	Police Lines	32° 59' 20.18" N,70° 36' 32.87" E
254	Tirah	Khyber Agency	N/A	Akakhel Khyber Agency	34° 1' 15.97" N,71° 17' 14.72" E
255	Police Station	Balakot	KPK	Police Station Balakot	34° 32' 60.00" N,73° 20' 60.00" E
256	Nishat Chowk	Mingora	KPK	Nishat Chowk	34° 46' 18.31" N,72° 21' 36.71" E
257	Police Station	Karak	KPK	Police Station Karak	33° 6' 37.72" N,71° 5' 28.95" E
258	Thal	Hangu	KPK	Thal	33° 22' 1.65" N,70° 32' 50.34" E

259	S.I.A Office	Lahore	Punjab	Model Town	31° 28' 39.85" N,74° 19' 45.91" E
260	Old Bara	Old Bara Area	FATA	Old Bara Area	
261	R.A Bazar	Lahore	Punjab	R.A Bazar	31° 30' 21.56" N,74° 23' 6.17" E
262	Checkpost	Mingora	KPK	Outside District Courts	34° 46' 25.13" N,72° 21' 35.64" E
263	Lagharai Area	Bajaur Agency	N/A	Bajaur Agency	34° 51' 24.85" N,71° 25' 47.77" E
264	Tank	Tank	KPK	Tank	32° 12' 51.47" N,70° 22' 39.83" E
265	US Consulate	Peshawar	KPK	Saddar Area	34° 0' 53.91" N,71° 34' 49.76" E
266	Timergarah	Lower Dir	KPK	Timargarah Rest House Lower Dir	34° 49' 41.00" N,71° 50' 27.00" E
267	Civil Hospital	Quetta	Balochistan	Civil Hospital Jinnah Road	30° 10' 58.70" N,66° 59' 55.44" E
268	IDPs Registration Centre	Kohat	KPK	Near Kacha Pakha	33° 35' 0.24" N,71° 25' 59.59" E
269	Police Station	Kohat	KPK	Belly Tang Police Station	33° 35' 0.24" N,71° 25' 59.59" E
270	Qissa Khwani Bazar	Peshawar	KPK	Qissa Khwani Bazar	34° 0' 28.47" N,71° 34' 12.47" E
271	Checkpost	Peshawar	KPK	Warsak Road Mathra Police Station	34° 1' 34.57" N,71° 32' 5.81" E

272	Plaza	Mingora	KPK	Sohrab Khan Chowk	34° 46' 20.24" N,72° 21' 24.71" E
273	Worship Places Of Ahmadis	Lahore	Punjab	Garhi Shahu And Model Town	31° 33' 16.58" N,74° 21' 25.77" E
274	Data Darbar	Lahore	Punjab	Data Darbar	31° 34' 44.29" N,74° 18' 17.07" E
275	Yakkaghund	Mohmand Agency	N/A	Yakkaghund	34° 33' 55.78" N,71° 28' 38.74" E
276	Kohat District	Kohat	KPK	Kohat district, kpk	
277	Imambargah	Sargodha	Punjab	Darul Uloom Muhammadia Madrassa And Imambargah Block 19	32° 5' 1.47" N,72° 40' 18.70" E
278	Outside Ministers House	Nowshera	KPK	Khan Sher Garhi Area	34° 0' 57.08" N,71° 58' 31.63" E
279	Near F.C Chowk	Peshawar	KPK	F.C Chowk Near Deans Trade Center	34° 0' 53.91" N,71° 34' 49.76" E
280	Mosque	Wana	N/A	Wana	32° 18' 17.00" N,69° 34' 13.00" E
281	Imambargah	Lahore	Punjab	Karbala Gamay Shah N5	31° 33' 16.58" N,74° 21' 25.77" E
282	Muslimabad	Mardan	KPK	Muslimabad Area of Madran district	
283	Meezan Chowk	Quetta	Balochistan	Meezan Chowk	30° 10' 58.70" N,66° 59' 55.44" E

284	Police Station	LakkiMarwat	KPK	Lakki City Police Station	32° 36' 19.00" N,70° 54' 52.00" E
285	Ministers House	Quetta	Balochistan	Railway Housing Society	30° 10' 58.70" N,66° 59' 55.44" E
286	Abdullah Shah Ghazi Shrine	Karachi	Sindh	Shahrah e Firdousi Clifton	24° 48' 38.24" N,67° 1' 49.59" E
287	Jabukhel	LakkiMarwat	KPK	Jabukhel	32° 32' 9.71" N,70° 40' 0.78" E
288	Police Line	Swabi	KPK	Swabi Police Line	34° 7' 0.00" N,72° 28' 0.00" E
289	Mosque	Darra Adamkhel	N/A	Wali Muhammad Khan Mosque Akhorwal	33° 41' 7.30" N,71° 30' 51.29" E
290	C.I.D Building	Karachi	Sindh	Near Chief Ministers House	24° 51' 41.26" N,67° 0' 35.78" E
291	Khai Gala	Rawalakot	N/A	Khai Gala	33° 50' 47.40" N,73° 49' 43.22" E
292	Shakai	Shakai Village	FATA	Shakai Village	
293	Milad Chowk	Bannu	KPK	Milad Chowk	32° 59' 10.00" N,70° 36' 15.00" E
294	Political Administration Office	Mohmand Agency	N/A	Ghalanai Area	34° 33' 55.78" N,71° 28' 38.74" E
295	Sariab Pattak	Quetta	Balochistan	Sariab Pattak	30° 10' 58.70" N,66° 59' 55.44" E
296	Bus Stand	Kohat	KPK	Teerah Bazar	33° 35' 0.24" N,71° 25' 59.59" E

297	Al Zohra Hospital	Hangu	KPK	Kalay Area	33° 31' 48.00" N,71° 3' 36.00" E
298	Mall Road	Peshawar	KPK	Near Missionary School	33° 59' 58.61" N,71° 32' 10.14" E
299	Entrance Of Imam Bargah	Rawalpindi	Punjab	Highway Link Darbar Road	33° 38' 26.18" N,73° 6' 13.35" E
300	Food Distribution Centre	Bajaur Agency	N/A	Khar	34° 44' 24.00" N,71° 31' 48.00" E
301	Near CMH Road	Muzaffarabad	N/A	CMH Road	34° 21' 34.87" N,73° 28' 15.79" E
302	Mosque	Bannu	KPK	Near Meeryan Police Station	32° 59' 10.00" N,70° 36' 15.00" E
303	Near Urdu Bazar	Lahore	Punjab	Gamay Shah And Data Darbar Road	31° 34' 29.08" N,74° 18' 34.64" E
304	N/A	Karachi	Sindh	N/A	24° 51' 41.26" N,67° 0' 35.78" E
305	Kohat Road	Khar	FATA	Khar, Bajaur Agency	
306	Kohat Road	Peshawar	KPK	Near Kohat Bus Stand	34° 0' 12.01" N,71° 33' 36.41" E
307	Punjab Regiment Centre	Mardan	KPK	Punjab Regiment Centre	34° 12' 13.73" N,72° 2' 16.54" E
308	Batkhela	Malakand	KPK	Batkhela	34° 37' 12.00" N,71° 58' 12.00" E
309	Near Police Station	Bannu	KPK	N/A	32° 59' 10.00" N,70° 36' 15.00" E

310	Bypass Road	Hangu	KPK	Aliabad Area	33° 31' 27.38'' N,71° 3' 51.59'' E
311	Adezai	Peshawar	KPK	Adezai Village Mattani	33° 47' 32.71'' N,71° 33' 44.56'' E
312	Doaba Police Station	Hangu	KPK	Thall Hangu Road	33° 25' 34.05'' N,70° 44' 25.62'' E
313	Swabi Interexchange	Swabi	KPK	Peshawar Islamabad Motorway	34° 7' 0.00'' N,72° 28' 0.00'' E
314	Near DCO Office	Charsadda	KPK	Nowshera Road	34° 8' 57.96'' N,71° 44' 34.01'' E
315	Khalid Plaza	Darra Adamkhel	N/A	Darra Adamkhel Bazaar	33° 41' 7.30'' N,71° 30' 51.29'' E
316	Sakhi Sarwar Shrine	Dera Ghazi Khan	Punjab	Sakhi Sarwar Shrine	29° 58' 45.00'' N,70° 18' 21.00'' E
317	Munda Bazar	Lower Dir	KPK	Munda Area	34° 50' 43.19'' N,71° 54' 16.43'' E
318	DIG House	Quetta	Balochistan	Gulistan Road	30° 10' 58.70'' N,66° 59' 55.44'' E
319	Salarzai Area	Bajaur Agency	KPK	Salarzai	34° 51' 24.85'' N,71° 25' 47.77'' E
320	F.C Headquarters	Shabqadar	KPK	F.C Headquarters	34° 13' 2.00'' N,71° 33' 20.00'' E
321	Near MCB Bank	Taunsa Sharif	Punjab	Main Bazar	30° 42' 20.00'' N,70° 39' 28.00'' E
322	C.I.D Building	Peshawar	KPK	G.T Road	34° 0' 24.40'' N,71° 31' 58.85'' E

323	Checkpoint Outside Police Station	Hangu	KPK	Near Hangu Police Chief Office	33° 32' 11.53" N,71° 3' 56.36" E
324	Market	Bajaur Agency	N/A	Salarzai Village	34° 51' 24.85" N,71° 25' 47.77" E
325	Bakery	Nowshera	KPK	Mall Road	34° 0' 57.08" N,71° 58' 31.63" E
326	Khyber Super Market	Peshawar	KPK	Khyber Super Market	33° 58' 42.34" N,71° 26' 6.81" E
327	Silk Bank	Islamabad	Punjab	Sector I-8	33° 40' 5.03" N,73° 4' 22.77" E
328	Police Station	Dera Ismail Khan	KPK	Kolachi Town	31° 49' 0.00" N,70° 55' 0.00" E
329	Battagram	Mansehra	KPK	Battagram	34° 13' 7.00" N,71° 37' 33.00" E
330	Kotki	Kotki Area	FATA	Kotki Area	
331	Near Checkpost	South Waziristan	FATA	Chak Malai South Waziristan	51° 30' 12.11" N,0° 7' 39.45" W
332	Danish Kol bazar	Momand Agency	FATA	Pandyai Area in Mohmand Agency	
333	Lahori Gate	Peshawar	KPK	Lahore Gate, Gulbahar, Peshawer	
334	Ghundai	Ghundai Area	FATA	Ghundai, Jamrud	
335	Quetta	Quetta	Balochistan	Quetta	
336	Near Checkpost	Peshawar	KPK	Lakki Marwat	32° 36' 19.00" N,70° 54' 52.00" E

337	D.I.G F.C House	Quetta	Balochistan	Anscumb Road Near Quetta Kacheri	30° 10' 58.70" N,66° 59' 55.44" E
338	Jandol	Lower Dir	KPK	Jandol, Lower Dir	
339	Darakhshan	Karachi	Sindh	Darakhsan Area of Karachi	
340	Risalpur	Nowshera	KPK	Risalpur Police Station, Nowshera District	
341	Malikabad	Swabi	KPK	Malikabad Area of Swabi District	
342	Clifton	Karachi	Sindh	Sea View at Clifton in Karachi	
343	Gulisatn e Johar	Karachi	Sindh	Block 13	24° 55' 34.66" N,67° 7' 49.80" E
344	Kohat Road	Bannu	KPK	Tochi Scouts checkpost	
345	Arbab Karam Khan Road	Quetta	Balochistan	Arbab Karam Khan Road	
346	Near Gorali Area	Gujrat	Punjab	G.T Road	32° 31' 37.35" N,74° 5' 45.96" E
347	District Police Office	Dera Ismail Khan	KPK	District Police Office	31° 49' 0.00" N,70° 55' 0.00" E
348	Akora Khattak	Nowshera	KPK	Akora Khattak Area	
349	Pakha Ghulam Area	Peshawar	KPK	Ring Road	34° 2' 16.63" N,71° 36' 26.13" E

350	Market Area	Upper Dir	KPK	Dir Town	35° 11' 51.58" N,71° 52' 29.72" E
351	Kurmi bazaar, Main Bazar	Parachinar	N/A	Main Bazar	33° 53' 57.00" N,70° 6' 3.00" E
352	Circular Road	Peshawar	KPK	Circular Road Police Station	
353	Tirah Valley	Tirah Valley	FATA	Tirah Valley	
354	Charsadda	Peshawar	KPK	Kangra	34° 10' 35.23" N,71° 35' 8.19" E
355	Commissionery Bazar	Dera Ismail Khan	KPK	Commissionery Bazar	31° 49' 42.76" N,70° 54' 6.76" E
356	Badhaber	Peshawar	KPK	Badhaber	33° 54' 44.00" N,71° 33' 17.93" E
357	Pishtakhara	Peshawar	KPK	Near Bara Road	33° 57' 8.65" N,71° 29' 50.80" E
358	Mosque	Khyber Agency	N/A	Akka Khel Bara	34° 1' 15.97" N,71° 17' 14.72" E
359	Malir	Karachi	Sindh	Malir Area of Karachi	
360	Market	Bajaur Agency	N/A	Main Market Khar	34° 51' 24.85" N,71° 25' 47.77" E
361	Gulbela	Charsadda	KPK	Gulbela, Charsadda Road, Daudzai	
362	Bazidkhel chowk, Badhaber	Peshawar	KPK	Bazidkhel Chowk Kohat Road	33° 54' 44.00" N,71° 33' 17.93" E

363	Jinnah Town	Quetta	Balochistan	Near BUITEMS, Jinnah Town Campus	
364	Near Hazar Ganji	Quetta	Balochistan	Hazar Ganji	30° 2' 28.00" N,66° 52' 2.00" E
365	Police Station	Bannu	KPK	Old City Police station	32° 59' 10.00" N,70° 36' 15.00" E
366	Speen Tall	Qrakzai Agency	FATA	Orakzai Agency	
367	Minhas PAF base	Attock	Punjab	Kamra, Attock	
368	Near Checkpost	Quetta	Balochistan	Quetta	30° 10' 58.70" N,66° 59' 55.44" E
369	Near UNHCR Office	Peshawar	KPK	University Town	33° 59' 31.80" N,71° 29' 53.54" E
370	Kashmir Chowk	Parachinar	N/A	Kashmir Chowk	33° 53' 57.00" N,70° 6' 3.00" E
371	Tor Khel Bazaar	Darra Adamkhel	N/A	Tor Khel Bazaar	33° 44' 3.78" N,71° 30' 53.15" E
372	Daggar	Buner	KPK	Daggar	32° 55' 45.06" N,72° 56' 9.93" E
373	Qissa Khwani Bazar	Peshawar	KPK	Qissa Khwani Bazar	34° 0' 29.07" N,71° 34' 31.64" E
374	Rangers Headquarters	Karachi	Sindh	North Nazimabad	24° 55' 60.00" N,67° 1' 60.00" E
375	Haleemzai Tehsil	Mohmand Agency	N/A	Ghaiba Khwar	34° 33' 55.78" N,71° 28' 38.74" E

376	Near ImamBargah	Rawalpindi	Punjab	Misrial Road	33° 36' 12.42" N,72° 59' 50.48" E
377	Commissionery Bazar	Dera Ismail Khan	KPK	Commissionery Bazar Near Mohalla Qasaban	31° 49' 0.00" N,70° 55' 0.00" E
378	Rustam Bazar	South Waziristan	N/A	Rustam Bazar Wana	32° 18' 17.00" N,69° 34' 13.00" E
379	Checkpoint	Bannu	KPK	Banuu Police Station	32° 59' 10.00" N,70° 36' 15.00" E
380	Checkpoint Near Army Camp	Wana	N/A	Zaree Noor Army Camp Waziristan	32° 18' 17.00" N,69° 34' 13.00" E
381	Police Station	Bannu	KPK	Kakki Police Station	32° 59' 10.00" N,70° 36' 15.00" E
382	Bazaar area	Peshawar	KPK	Qissa Khawani Bazaar	32° 59' 10.00" N,70° 36' 15.00" E
383	Takhta Band Road, Mingora	Mingora	KPK	Tablighi Markaz in Takhta Band Road, Mingora City, Swat District	
384	Alamdar Road	Quetta	Balochistan	Rehmatullah Chowk	30° 10' 58.70" N,66° 59' 55.44" E
385	In Front Of Two Mosque	Hangu	KPK	Pat Bazar Area	33° 31' 48.00" N,71° 3' 36.00" E
386	Army Camp	LakkiMarwat	KPK	Sarai Nourang	32° 36' 19.00" N,70° 54' 52.00" E
387	Karachi	Karachi	Sindh	Karachi	

388	security checkpost in SpinThall Area	Hangu	KPK	Spin Thall, Hangu	
389	Miryan	Bannu	KPK	Miryan Police Station of Bannu District	
390	Orakzai Agency	North Waziristan	N/A	N/A	33° 41' 50.18" N,71° 8' 41.47" E
391	Market	Quetta	Balochistan	Hazara Town Kirani Road	30° 10' 58.70" N,66° 59' 55.44" E
392	Peshawar Cantt	Peshawar	KPK	Khyber House, khyber agency	
393	Peshawar	Peshawar	KPK	N/A	34° 0' 53.91" N,71° 34' 49.76" E
394	Peshawar	Peshawar	KPK	N/A	34° 0' 53.91" N,71° 34' 49.76" E
395	Court Room	Peshawar	KPK	G.T Road	34° 0' 24.40" N,71° 31' 58.85" E
396	TTP headquarters of the AL in Bagh Area	Tirah Valley	FATA	Bagh Area, Tirah Valley	
397	Checkpost	Miranshah	N/A	North Waziristan	33° 0' 0.00" N,70° 3' 54.00" E
398	Saddar Area	Peshawar	KPK	Near US Conslate	34° 0' 53.91" N,71° 34' 49.76" E
399	Market	Mardan	KPK	Katlang Area	34° 21' 34.80" N,72° 4' 24.53" E

400	Bannu	Bannu	KPK	Jani Khel Area	32° 59' 10.00" N,70° 36' 15.00" E
401	Quetta	Quetta	Balochistan	Saryab Area	30° 10' 58.70" N,66° 59' 55.44" E
402	Khyber Agency	Khyber Agency	N/A	Landi Kotal Area	34° 1' 15.97" N,71° 17' 14.72" E
403	Peshawar	Peshawar	KPK	Mattni Bazar	34° 0' 53.91" N,71° 34' 49.76" E
404	Charsadda	Peshawar	KPK	N/A	34° 8' 57.96" N,71° 44' 34.01" E
405	Saidgai	N/A	FATA	Checkpoint, Saidgai Area, NWA	
406	At Political Rally	Peshawar	KPK	Peshawar	34° 0' 53.91" N,71° 34' 49.76" E
407	Ladha	South Wazirisatn	N/A	N/A	32° 19' 12.85" N,69° 51' 35.07" E
408	Outside Hospital	Bajaur Agency	N/A	Khar	34° 44' 24.00" N,71° 31' 48.00" E
409	Ghilzai Road	Quetta	Balochistan	Near Pir Mohammad Khan Road	30° 10' 58.70" N,66° 59' 55.44" E
410	Peshawar	Peshawar	KPK	Mansehra	34° 0' 53.91" N,71° 34' 49.76" E
411	Karachi	Karachi	Sindh	N/A	24° 49' 32.42" N,67° 7' 54.62" E
412	Quetta	Quetta	Balochistan	N/A	30° 10' 58.70" N,66° 59' 55.44" E

413	Karachi	Karachi	Sindh	N/A	24° 51' 41.26" N,67° 0' 35.78" E
414	Universty Road	Peshawar	KPK	University Road	34° 0' 53.91" N,71° 34' 49.76" E
415	Police Station	Bannu	KPK	N/A	32° 59' 10.00" N,70° 36' 15.00" E
416	Swabi	Peshawar	KPK	N/A	34° 7' 0.00" N,72° 28' 0.00" E
417	Zarghoon Road	Quetta	Balochistan	Near Ptcl Office	30° 10' 58.70" N,66° 59' 55.44" E
418	Mosque	Malakand	KPK	N/A	34° 30' 10.95" N,71° 54' 16.43" E
419	Sher Garh	Mardan	KPK	Sher Garh	34° 20' 49.00" N,71° 54' 2.00" E
420	South Waziristan	South Waziristan	N/A	Wana Dargai Area	32° 19' 12.85" N,69° 51' 35.07" E
421	Peshawar	Peshawar	KPK	N/A	34° 0' 53.91" N,71° 34' 49.76" E
422	Checkpost	Swabi	KPK	N/A	34° 7' 0.00" N,72° 28' 0.00" E
423	Peshawar	Peshawar	KPK	Imamia Colony	34° 0' 53.91" N,71° 34' 49.76" E
424	Quetta	Quetta	Balochistan	Kharotabad Area	30° 10' 58.70" N,66° 59' 55.44" E
425	Peshawar	Peshawar	KPK	N/A	34° 0' 53.91" N,71° 34' 49.76" E

426	Universty Bus	Quetta	Balochistan	Sardar Bahdur Khan Women Universty Brewery Road	30° 10' 58.70" N,66° 59' 55.44" E
427	BMC Hospital	Quetta	Balochistan	Bolan Medical Complex Brewery Road	30° 10' 58.70" N,66° 59' 55.44" E
428	Imambargah	Peshawar	KPK	Peshawar	34° 0' 53.91" N,71° 34' 49.76" E
429	Kuchlac	Quetta	Balochistan	Kuchlac	30° 21' 43.28" N,66° 57' 10.83" E
430	Near Imambargah of Aliabad area, Hazara Town	Quetta	Balochistan	Aliabad, Hazara Town, Quetta	
431	Near ImamBargah	Quetta	Balochistan	Kirani Road	30° 10' 58.70" N,66° 59' 55.44" E
432	Checkpost	North Waziristan	FATA	Datta Khel	33° 8' 60.00" N,70° 25' 60.00" E
433	Border	Chaman	Balochistan	Pak Afghan Border Chaman	30° 55' 20.00" N,66° 26' 41.00" E
434	Torha Warhai	Hangu	KPK	Torha Warhai, Doaba Bazaar, Hangu	
435	Chaman Town	Chaman	Balochistan	Chaman Town, Qilla Abdullah, Balochistan	

436	ISI Office	Sukkur	Sindh	Barrage Colony	27° 42' 23.77" N,68° 50' 53.51" E
437	Market	Parachinar	N/A	Kurram Agency	33° 53' 57.00" N,70° 6' 3.00" E
438	Police Line	Quetta	Balochistan	Gulistan Road	30° 10' 58.70" N,66° 59' 55.44" E
439	Police Line	Ladha	KPK	N/A	34° 0' 53.91" N,71° 34' 49.76" E
440	Quetta	Quetta	Balochistan	N/A	30° 10' 58.70" N,66° 59' 55.44" E
441	All Saints Church	Peshawar	KPK	All Saints Church	34° 0' 53.91" N,71° 34' 49.76" E
442	SpinThall Area	Hangu	KPK	Headquarter of Mullah Nabi Hanfi Group, spinthal	
443	Friendship Gate	Chaman	Balochistan	Pak Afghan Border Chaman	30° 55' 20.00" N,66° 26' 41.00" E
444	SpinThall Area	Orakzai Agency	N/A	SpinThall Area	33° 41' 50.18" N,71° 8' 41.47" E
445	Kohat	Kohat	KPK	N/A	33° 35' 0.24" N,71° 25' 59.59" E
446	Wana	South Waziristan	N/A	South Waziristan	32° 18' 17.00" N,69° 34' 13.00" E
447	Ministers House	Dera Ismail Khan	KPK	Kullachi	31° 55' 43.00" N,70° 27' 33.00" E

448	River Kurram Bridge	Bannu	KPK	River Kurram Bridge	32° 59' 10.00" N,70° 36' 15.00" E
449	Mirali	North Waziristan	FATA	Mirali North Waziristan	32° 58' 12.07" N,70° 16' 39.30" E
450	Gulberg Town Karachi	Karachi	Sindh	Ancholi Area	24° 51' 41.26" N,67° 0' 35.78" E
451	Quetta	Quetta	Balochistan	Lehri Area	28° 29' 26.64" N,65° 5' 44.80" E
452	Peshawar	Peshawar	KPK	Badhber Village	33° 54' 44.00" N,71° 33' 17.93" E
453	Imambargah	Rawalpindi	Punjab	Imambargah Asna Asharia Near Noor Khan Airbase	33° 35' 54.22" N,73° 2' 38.89" E
454	Quetta	Quetta	Balochistan	Pashtoonabad Area	30° 10' 58.70" N,66° 59' 55.44" E
455	Akhtarabad	Quetta	Balochistan	Bypass Road	30° 10' 58.70" N,66° 59' 55.44" E
456	Outside government school Ibrahimzai area	Hangu	KPK	IbrahimZai Area of Hangu District	
457	Lyari Expressway	Karachi	Sindh	Near Essa Nagri at Lyari Expressway	
458	Bunnu Garrison	Bannu	KPK	Bannu Garrison	32° 59' 10.00" N,70° 36' 15.00" E
459	Near GHQ	Rawalpindi	Punjab	Near R A Bazar	33° 35' 54.22" N,73° 2' 38.89" E

460	Kohat Road	Peshawar	KPK	Kohat road	34° 0' 12.01" N,71° 33' 36.41" E
461	Rengers Headquarters	Karachi	Sindh	North Nazimabad	24° 55' 60.00" N,67° 1' 60.00" E
462	Resturant	Peshawar	KPK	Kocha Risaldar	34° 0' 21.38" N,71° 34' 12.93" E
463	Khanewal Town	Khanewal	Punjab	Khanewal Town, Khanewal	
464	Suburban Village	Peshawar	KPK	Ring Road	34° 0' 21.38" N,71° 34' 12.93" E
465	Latif Town	Karachi	Sindh	Razzakabad Police Training Center, Shah Latif Town, Karachi	
466	Qayumabad	Karachi	Sindh	Qayumabad	24° 51' 41.26" N,67° 0' 35.78" E
467	Checkpost Outside Iranian Consulate	Peshawar	KPK	University Town	34° 0' 53.91" N,71° 34' 49.76" E
468	Session Court	Islamabad	Punjab	Session Court Islamabad	33° 43' 45.80" N,73° 5' 35.33" E
469	Battathal Area	Peshawar	KPK	Near sarband	34° 0' 53.91" N,71° 34' 49.76" E
470	Tailor Shop	Karachi	Sindh	Sabzi Mandi Area	24° 51' 41.26" N,67° 0' 35.78" E

471	Near Mosque	Khyber Agency	N/A	Shah Tehmas Khan Stadium	34° 1' 15.97" N,71° 17' 14.72" E
472	Fateh Jang Road	Rawalpindi	Punjab	Fateh Jang Road	33° 35' 54.22" N,73° 2' 38.89" E
473	Jinnah Airport	Karachi	Sindh	Airport Road	24° 51' 41.26" N,67° 0' 35.78" E
474	Boya Checkpost	North Waziristan	FATA	Datta Khel Road, NWA	
475	Near Hospital	North Waziristan	N/A	Spinwarm	32° 19' 12.85" N,69° 51' 35.07" E
476	Saddar Road	Peshawar	KPK	Saddar Road	34° 0' 5.52" N,71° 32' 52.54" E
477	Hazara Town Market	Quetta	Balochistan	Aliabad Hazara Town	30° 10' 55.18" N,66° 57' 25.57" E
478	Pir Mela	Tirah Valley	FATA	Pir Mela Area of Tirah Valley in Khyber Agency	
479	Meckongi Road	Quetta	Balochistan	Near Archar Road	30° 11' 32.90" N,67° 0' 51.44" E
480	Wagah Border	Lahore	Punjab	Pakistan India Border	28° 7' 17.98" N,71° 55' 45.65" E
481	Army Public School	Peshawar	KPK	Warsak Road	34° 1' 35.13" N,71° 32' 5.53" E
482	Ismailzai	Zhob	Balochistan	Gawal, Ismailzai area	
483	Imambargah	Shikarpur	Sindh	Maula Karballa lakhi Dar	27° 56' 60.00" N,68° 39' 0.00" E

					Imamia Imambargah	34° 0' 53.91" N,71° 34'
484	Imambargah	Peshawar	KPK		Hayatabad	49.76" E
485	Near Police Line	Lahore	Punjab		Qila Gujar Singh Area	31° 33' 16.58" N,74° 21' 25.77" E
486	Qasre-sina Imambargah, kurri road	Rawalpindi	Punjab		Kurri Road, New shakrial, Rawalpindi	33° 35' 54.22" N,73° 2' 38.89" E
487	Outside Church	Lahore	Punjab		Youhanaabad	31° 33' 16.58" N,74° 21' 25.77" E
488	Roadside	Karachi	Sindh		Qalandria Chowk North Nazimabad	24° 51' 41.26" N,67° 0' 35.78" E

		Bomber(s)				About Bomb		
No.	Time	No.	Susp. Age	Other Weapon(s)	Origin/ Identity	Type	Weight - KG	No.
1	N/A	2	N/A	N/A	N/A	By Vehicle	N/A	2
2	N/A	1	N/A	N/A	N/A	N/A	N/A	1
3	7:45AM	1	N/A	N/A	N/A	By Vehicle	2.5kg	1
4	11:10PM	1	N/A	N/A	N/A	By Vehicle	N/A	1
5	N/A	3	N/A	Automatic weapons & Handgrenade	N/A	N/A	N/A	1
6	N/A	1	N/A	N/A	N/A	N/A	N/A	1
7	1:42 PM	2	30s	N/A		By Vehicle	40KG Each	2
8	N/A	1	Mid 20s	N/A	N/A	By Foot	N/A	1
9	1:17	1	N/A	N/A	N/A	By Foot	2kg	1
10	N/A	1	N/A	N/A	N/A	By Foot	N/A	1
11	7:20PM	1	N/A	N/A	N/A	By Foot	N/A	1
12	1:27PM	1	N/A	N/A	N/A	N/A	N/A	1
13	5:55PM	1	28	N/A	N/A	By Foot	N/A	1
14	11:45PM	1	N/A	N/A	N/A	N/A	N/A	1

15	N/A	2	N/A	N/A	N/A	While planting	N/A	N/A
16	N/A	1	N/A	N/A	N/A	By Foot	N/A	1
17	N/A	3	N/A	N/A	N/A	By Foot	N/A	1
18	N/A	1	N/A	N/A	N/A	Suspected	N/A	1
19	9:35AM	1	N/A	N/A	N/A	By Foot	N/A	3
20	9:00AM	1	N/A	N/A	N/A	By Vehicle	N/A	1
21	7:00PM	1	N/A	N/A	N/A	By Foot	5KG	1
22	10:30AM	2	N/A	N/A	N/A	By Vehicle	N/A	1
23	N/A	1	N/A	N/A	N/A	By Vehicle	N/A	1
24	N/A	1	25	N/A	N/A	By Bicycle	N/A	1
25	8:30AM	1	30	N/A	N/A	By Foot	N/A	1
26	7:30AM	1	N/A	N/A	N/A	By Foot	N/A	1
27	N/A	1	N/A	Handgrenade & Pistol	Uzbek	By Foot	N/A	1
28	N/A		N/A	Fighter Plane	NATO forces	N/A	N/A	1
29	10:30AM	1	N/A	N/A	N/A	By Vehicle	N/A	1
30	2:37 PM	1	N/A	N/A	N/A	By Foot	N/A	1
31	8:40 PM	1	N/A	N/A	N/A	By Vehicle	N/A	1
32	N/A	1	15	N/A	N/A	By Foot	N/A	1
33	6:17 AM	1	20	Hand Grenade, Pistol	Uzbek	N/A	N/A	1
34	12:15 PM	1	N/A	N/A	N/A	By Vehicle	N/A	1
35	9:10 PM	1	N/A	Hand Grenade, Guns	N/A	By Vehicle	N/A	1
36	11:05 AM	1	20	N/A	N/A	By Foot	2	1
37	12:00 PM	1	22	N/A	N/A	By Foot	N/A	1
38	4:00 PM	1	33	N/A	Afghan	By Foot	N/A	1
39								
40	12:55PM	1	N/A	N/A	N/A	By Vehicle	N/A	1
41	10:25AM	1	N/A	N/A	N/A	By Vehicle	N/A	1
42	4:30PM	1	N/A	Pistol	N/A	By Foot	N/A	1
43	N/A	3	N/A	Remote Control Bomb	N/A	By Foot	N/A	2

44	N/A	1	N/A	N/A	N/A	By Vehicle	N/A	1
45	4:00 PM	1	N/A	N/A	N/A	By Foot	N/A	1
46	N/A	2	N/A	N/A	N/A	By Vehicle	N/A	2
47	8:30 (?)	1	N/A	N/A	N/A	By Foot	N/A	1
48	N/A	1	N/A	N/A	N/A	By Foot	N/A	1
49	N/A	N/A	N/A	N/A	N/A	By Vehicle	N/A	N/A
50	7.30am	1	N/A	N/A	N/A	By Vehicle	N/A	1
51	N/A	1	N/A	N/A	N/A	By Foot	N/A	1
52	N/A	1	N/A	N/A	N/A	By Vehicle	N/A	1
53	5;25PM	1	20	N/A	N/A	By Foot	N/A	1
54	N/A	1	N/A	N/A	N/A	By Foot	N/A	1
55	N/A	1	N/A	N/A	N/A	By Vehicle	N/A	1
56	N/A	1	N/A	N/A	N/A	By Vehicle	N/A	1
57	N/A	1	N/A	N/A	N/A	By Foot	N/A	1
58	N/A	1	N/A	N/A	N/A	By Vehicle	N/A	1
59	N/A	1	N/A	N/A	N/A	By Vehicle	N/A	1
60	9:AM	1	N/A	N/A	N/A	By Vehicle	N/A	1
61	N/A	1	N/A	N/A	N/A	By Vehicle	N/A	1
62	N/A	2	N/A	N/A	N/A	By Vehicle	N/A	1
63	N/A	1	N/A	N/A	N/A	N/A	N/A	1
64		1	N/A	N/A	N/A			
65	10:00am	2	N/A	N/A	N/A	By Vehicle	N/A	1
66	7:15AM	1	N/A	N/A	N/A	N/A	N/A	1
67	7:20AM	1	N/A	N/A	N/A	By Motor Bike	N/A	1
68	N/A	1	15	N/A	N/A	By Foot	N/A	1
69	8:00PM	1	N/A	N/A	N/A	By Vehicle	N/A	1
70	N/A	1	N/A	N/A	N/A	By Vehicle	N/A	1
71	N/A	1	N/A	N/A	N/A	By Foot	N/A	1
72	12:00PM	2	N/A	N/A	N/A	By Foot	N/A	2
73	2:45PM	1	N/A	N/A	N/A	By Vehicle	N/A	1
74	11;50 AM	1	N/A	N/A	N/A	By Foot	N/A	1
75	7:10AM	1	N/A	N/A	N/A	By Motor Bike	N/A	1
76	3:45PM	1	23	N/A	N/A	By Foot	5 KG	1
77	7:40AM	1	N/A	N/A	N/A	By Vehicle	N/A	1

78	7:50AM	1	N/A	N/A	N/A	By Vehicle	N/A	1
79	N/A	1	30	N/A	N/A	By Foot	N/A	1
80	11:15Am	1	N/A	N/A	N/A	By Vehicle	15Kg	1
81	7:26Am	1	21	N/A	Pashtun	By Vehicle	N/A	1
82	5:00PM	2	24	N/A	N/A	By Foot	N/A	2
83	9:25AM	1	N/A	N/A	N/A	By Bicycle	N/A	1
84	12:00PM	1	16	N/A	N/A	By Foot	5KG	1
85	N/A	1	N/A	N/A	N/A	By Foot	6kG	1
86	6:00PM	1	N/A	N/A	N/A	By Vehicle	N/A	1
87	5:00PM	1	N/A	Pistol	N/A	By Foot	5KG	1
88	11:15AM	1	N/A	N/A	N/A	By Vehicle	N/A	1
89	N/A	1	18	N/A	N/A	By Foot	15KG	1
90	10:30AM	3	13	N/A	N/A	By Foot	N/A	1
91	6:55PM	1	16	N/A	N/A	By Foot	10KG	1
92								
93	4:30PM	1	N\A	N/A	N/A	By Vehicle	N/A	1
94	7:30AM	1	N\A	N/A	N/A	By Motor Bike	N/A	1
95	N/A	1	N\A	N/A	N/A	By Foot	N/A	1
96	N/A	1	N\A	N/A	N/A	By Foot	N/A	1
97	12:55PM	1	N\A	N/A	N/A	By Vehicle	N/A	1
98	N/A	1	N\A	N/A	N/A	By Vehicle	N/A	1
99	N/A	1	N\A	N/A	N/A	By Vehicle	N/A	1
100	2.45PM	1	17	N/A	N/A	By Foot	N/A	1
101	8:00PM	1	N\A	N/A	N/A	By Foot	N/A	1
102	N/A	1	N\A	N/A	N/A	By Vehicle	N/A	1
103	N/A	1	20	N/A	N/A	By Foot	N/A	1
104	1:08PM	2	N/A	N/A	N/A	By Motor Bike	N/A	2
105	9:20AM	1	N/A	N/A	N/A	By Vehicle	50KG	N/A
106	9:21AM	2	N/A	N/A	N/A	By Vehicle	30 KG	2
107	N/A	1	N/A	N/A	N/A	By Foot	N/A	1
108	3:00PM	1	N/A	N/A	N/A	By Vehicle	N/A	1
109	N/A	1	18	Pistol	N/A	By Foot	N/A	1
110	8:40AM	1	N\A	N/A	N/A	By Foot	N/A	1
111	N/A	1	N\A	N/A	N/A	By Vehicle	N/A	1
112	8:00PM	1	N\A	N/A	N/A	By Foot	N/A	1

113	1:00PM	1	N\A	N/A	N/A	By Vehicle	20KG	1
114	7:45PM	1	33	N/A	N/A	By Foot	5KG	1
115	N/A	1	N/A	N/A	N/A	By Foot	N/A	1
116	11:34PM	1	21	N/A	N/A	By Motor Bike	4KG	1
117	N/A	1	16	N/A	N/A	By Foot	N/A	1
118	2:37PM	2	N/A	N/A	N/A	By Foot	N/A	2
119	N/A	1	N/A	N/A	N/A	By Foot	12KG	1
120	7:45AM	1	N/A	N/A	N/A	By Vehicle	100KG	1
121	N/A	2	N/A	N/A	N/A	By Vehicle	N/A	2
122	N/A	1	20	N/A	N/A	By Vehicle	??	1
123	N/A	1	N/A	N/A	N/A	By Vehicle	N/A	1
124	N/A	2	N/A	N/A	N/A	Foiled attempt of hostage	N/A	2
125	8:00PM	1	N/A	N/A	N/A	By Vehicle	N/A	1
126	N/A	1	N/A	N/A	N/A	By Vehicle	N/A	1
127	N/A	1	N/A	N/A	N/A	By Vehicle	N/A	1
128	N/A	1	21	N/A	Afghan	By Foot	5-8KG	1
129	N/A	3	N/A	N/A	N/A	Police Raid	N/A	N/A
130	4:00PM	1	20	N/A	N/A	By Foot	N/A	1
131	4:45PM	1	N/A	N/A	N/A	By Foot	N/A	1
132	12:45PM	1	20	N/A	N/A	By Vehicle	50-60KG	1
133	N/A	1	N/A	N/A	N/A	By Vehicle	N/A	1
134	N/A	1	N/A	N/A	N/A	By Vehicle	N/A	1
135	N/A	1	N/A	N/A	N/A	By Vehicle	N/A	1
136	N/A	1	N/A	N/A	N/A	By Vehicle	N/A	1
137	2:15PM	1	N/A	N/A	N/A	By Vehicle	N/A	1
138	N/A	1	23	N/A	N/A	By Foot	N/A	1
139	9:00AM	1	N\A	N/A	N/A	By Vehicle	N/A	1
140	N/A	1	N\A	N/A	N/A	By Vehicle	N/A	1
141	N/A	1	N\A	N/A	N/A	By Foot	N/A	1
142	N/A	1	N\A	N/A	N/A	By Vehicle	N/A	1
143	N/A	1	22	N/A	N/A	By Foot	7KG	1
144	N/A	1	N/A	N/A	N/A	By Vehicle	N/A	1
145	N/A	1	N/A	N/A	N/A	By Vehicle	N/A	1
146	N/A	1	N/A	N/A	N/A	By Foot	N/A	1

147	N/A	1	N/A	N/A	N/A	N/A	N/A	1
148	N/A	1	N/A	N/A	N/A	By Vehicle	N/A	1
149	N/A	1	N/A	N/A	N/A	By Vehicle	N/A	1
150	N/A	1	N/A	N/A	N/A	By Vehicle	N/A	1
151	N/A	1	N/A	N/A	N/A	By Foot	N/A	1
152	10:30AM	1	N/A	N/A	N/A	By Vehicle	N/A	1
153	N/A	1	N/A	N/A	N/A	N/A	N/A	1
154	7:30PM	1	21	N/A	N/A	By Foot	8-10KG	1
155	N/A	1	N/A	N/A	N/A	By Vehicle	N/A	1
156	N/A	1	N/A	N/A	N/A	By Vehicle	N/A	1
157	N/A	1	20	N/A	N/A	By Foot	12KG	1
158	8:15AM	1	N/A	N/A	N/A	By Vehicle	N/A	1
159	N/A	1	N/A	N/A	N/A	By Vehicle	N/A	1
160	10:05AM	1	17	N/A	N/A	By Foot	N/A	1
161	N/A	2	N/A	N/A	N/A	By Vehicle	N/A	1
162	N/A	1	N/A	N/A	N/A	By Foot	N/A	1
163	N/A	1	17	N/A	N/A	By Foot	N/A	1
164	N/A	2	N/A	Hand Grenade	N/A	By Foot	N/A	2
165	N/A	1	19	N/A	N/A	By Foot	10-15KG	1
166	N/A	1	N/A	Firing	N/A	By Foot	N/A	1
167	N/A	1	N/A	N/A	N/A	By Foot	N/A	1
168	N/A	1	N/A	N/A	N/A	By Foot	N/A	1
169	N/A	1	N/A	N/A	N/A	By Vehicle	N/A	1
170	N/A	1	N/A	N/A	N/A	By Foot	N/A	1
171	7.35PM	1	N/A	N/A	N/A	By Foot	7-8KG	1
172	N/A	1	N/A	N/A	N/A	By Vehicle	N/A	1
173	12.30PM	1	18	N/A	N/A	By Foot	N/A	1
174	N/A	1	N/A	N/A	N/A	By Vehicle	N/A	1
175	3:00PM	1	N/A	N/A	N/A	By Vehicle	N/A	1
176	N/A	1	N/A	N/A	N/A	By Vehicle	N/A	1
177	9:30AM	1	N/A	N/A	N/A	By Vehicle	N/A	1
178	N/A	1	N/A	N/A	N/A	By Vehicle	N/A	1
179	10:22AM	2	N/A	Ak47 & Handgrenade	N/A	By Vehicle	100KG	2
180	N/A	2	N/A	N/A	N/A	By Vehicle	160KG	1
181	N/A	1	N/A	N/A	N/A	By Foot	N/A	1
182	N/A	1	N/A	N/A	N/A	By Foot	N/A	1

183	8:35PM	1	23	N/A	N/A	By Foot	N/A	1
184	10:30PM	4	N/A	N/A	N/A	By Vehicle	500KG	1
185	N/A	1	N/A	Hand Grenade	N/A	By Foot	N/A	1
186	2:43PM	1	17	N/A	N/A	By Foot	20_24KG	1
187	2:40PM	1	N/A	Mortar Shells	N/A	By Vehicle	N/A	1
188	N/A	1	N/A	N/A	N/A	By Vehicle	N/A	1
189	6:00AM	1	18	N/A	N/A	By Foot	N/A	1
190	N/A	1	N/A	N/A	N/A	By Foot	N/A	1
191	N/A	1	N/A	N/A	N/A	By Foot	N/A	1
192	N/A	Multiple	N/A	Explosive Devices	N/A	By Vehicle	N/A	3
193	4:30PM	1	22	N/A	N/A	By motor Bike	N/A	1
194	N/A	1	16	N/A	N/A	By Foot	20KG	1
195	N/A	1	N/A	N/A	N/A	By Vehicle	N/A	1
196	N/A	1	N/A	N/A	N/A	By Motor Bike	N/A	1
197	10AM	1	N/A	N/A	N/A	By Vehicle	N/A	1
198	N/A	1	N/A	N/A	N/A	By Foot	N/A	1
199	7:00PM	1	N/A	N/A	N/A	By Vehicle	N/A	1
200	N/A	1	N/A	N/A	N/A	By Foot	N/A	1
201	N/A	1	15	N/A	N/A	By Foot	N/A	1
202	N/A	1	30	N/A	N/A	By Foot	10-12KG	1
203	N/A	1	N/A	N/A	N/A	By Motor Bike	N/A	1
204	N/A	1	N/A	N/A	N/A	By vehicle	N/A	1
205	N/A	1	N/A	N/A	N/A	By Vehicle	N/A	1
206	10:00AM	1	N/A	N/A	N/A	By Vehicle	150KG	1
207	N/A	1	18	N/A	N/A	By Foot	N/A	1
208	N/A	4	Teenager	Guns	N/A	N/A	N/A	1
209	11:35AM	1	N/A	Hand Grenade	N/A	By Vehicle	100KG	1
210	7:20AM	1	16	N/A	N/A	By Vehicle	150-180KG	1
211	N/A	1	N/A	N/A	N/A	By Vehicle	N/A	1
212	12:15PM	1	20	N/A	N/A	By Foot	8KG	1
213	12:16PM	1	N/A	N/A	N/A	By Vehicle	100KG	1
214	1:00PM	1	15	N/A	N/A	By Foot	N/A	1
215	8:00AM	1	20	N/A	N/A	By Vehicle	100KG	1

216	9:30AM	5	N/A	Hand Grenade	N/A	By Foot	N/A	3
217	12:45PM	1	N/A	N/A	N/A	By Vehicle	60-70KG	1
218	2:10PM	2	N/A	N/A	N/A	By Foot	16KG	2
219	7:00AM	1	N/A	N/A	N/A	By Foot	N/A	1
220	N/A	1	N/A	N/A	N/A	By Vehicle	N/A	1
221	10:40AM	1	N/A	N/A	N/A	By Foot	10-15KG	1
222	7:30PM	2	18	N/A	N/A	By Vehicle	20KG	1
223	9:30AM	1	20	N/A	N/A	By Foot	10KG	1
224	9:45AM	1	N/A	N/A	N/A	By Rickshaw	5-6KG	1
225	4:30PM	1	N/A	Mortar Shells	N/A	By Vehicle	40KG	1
226	6:40AM	1	N/A	N/A	N/A	By Vehicle	400KG	1
227	7:10AM	1	N/A	N/A	N/A	By Vehicle	200KG	1
228	4:15PM	1	N/A	N/A	N/A	By Vehicle	50-60KG	1
229	N/A	1	N/A	Artillery Shells	N/A	By Vehicle	250KG	1
230	10:10AM	1	17	N/A	N/A	By Foot	8-10KG	1
231	N/A	1	20	N/A	N/A	By Foot	8-10KG	1
232	1:35PM	1	17	N/A	N/A	By Foot	10-12KG	1
233	N/A	4	N/A	Hand Grenade	N/A	By Foot	N/A	2
234	8:42PM	1	N/A	N/A	N/A	N/A	N/A	1
235	12:55PM	1	16	N/A	N/A	By Foot	7-8KG	1
236	12:10PM	2	N/A	Hand Grenade	N/A	By Vehicle	800-1000KG	1
237	N/A	1	N/A	N/A	N/A	By Vehicle	1000KG	1
238	N/A	1	14	N/A	N/A	By Vehicle	N/A	1
239	1:30PM	2	N/A	N/A	N/A	By Vehicle	20KG	1
240	11:45AM	1	18	N/A	N/A	By Foot	8--10KG	1
241	11:57AM	1	23	N/A	N/A	By Motor Bike	8KG	1
242	10:18PM	1	18	N/A	N/A	By Foot	N/A	1
243	7:00PM	1	19	N/A	N/A	By Foot	N/A	1
244	N/A	1	N/A	N/A	N/A	By Foot	N/A	1
245	5:00PM	1	N/A	N/A	N/A	By Vehicle	250KG	1
246	6:50AM	1	N/A	N/A	N/A	By Foot	N/A	1
247	N/A	1	N/A	N/A	N/A	N/A	N/A	1
248	N/A	1	N/A	N/A	Irfan	During police raid	N/A	1

249	10:10AM	1	N/A	N/A	N/A	By Foot	N/A	1
250	N/A	1	N/A	N/A	N/A	By Vehicle	N/A	1
251	N/A	1	17	N/A	N/A	By Foot	N/A	1
252	N/A	1	18	N/A	N/A	By Vehicle	N/A	1
253	N/A	2	N/A	N/A	N/A	By Foot	N/A	2
254	N/A	1	N/A	N/A	N/A	By Vehicle	40KG	1
255	9:00AM	2	17	N/A	N/A	By Foot	N/A	1
256	4:20PM	1	N/A	N/A	N/A	By Foot	N/A	1
257	N/A	1	N/A	N/A	N/A	By Vehicle	180-200KG	1
258	N/A	1	17	N/A	N/A	By Vehicle	10-12KG	1
259	8:17AM	1	24	N/A	N/A	By Vehicle	600KG	1
260	N/A	1	N/A	N/A	N/A	N/A	N/A	1
261	12:45PM	2	19	N/A	N/A	By Foot	10-12KG Each	2
262	9:15AM	1	N/A	N/A	N/A	By Foot	14KG	1
263	N/A	1	N/A	N/A	N/A	By Foot	N/A	1
264	N/A	4	N/A	N/A	N/A	By Foot	N/A	1
265	1:19PM 1:31PM 1:33PM	5	N/A	Rockets And Handgrenade	N/A	By Foot / By Vehicle	N/A	3
266	12:00PM	1	15	N/A	N/A	By Foot	N/A	1
267	N/A	1	28	N/A	N/A	By Foot	15KG	1
268	11:55AM & 12:02PM	2	19	N/A	N/A	By Foot	8-10KG Each	2
269	7:15AM	1	N/A	N/A	N/A	By Vehicle	250KG	1
270	6:30PM	1	15	N/A	N/A	By Foot	6-8KG	1
271	4:05AM	1	N/A	N/A	N/A	By Vehicle	200KG	1
272	N/A	5	N/A	N/A	N/A	By Foot	15KG	1
273	N/A	7	N/A	Hand Grenade	N/A	By Foot	N/A	3
274	10:45PM	3	19	N/A	N/A	By Foot	20KG	3
275	9:30AM	2	N/A	N/A	N/A	By Motor Bike / By Vehicle	N/A	2
276	N/A	1	N/A	N/A	N/A	N/A	N/A	1
277	7:19PM	1	17	N/A	N/A	By Foot	N/A	1
278	N/A	1	N/A	N/A	N/A	By Foot	8-10KG	1

279	4:00PM	1	15	N/A	N/A	By Foot	8KG	1
280	N/A	1	N/A	N/A	N/A	By Foot	20KG	1
281	7:00PM 1st 7:13PM 2nd	3	N/A	N/A	N/A	By Foot	N/A	3
282	N/A	1	N/A	N/A	N/A	By Foot	N/A	1
283	N/A	1	28	N/A	N/A	By Foot	10-15KG	1
284	7:00AM	1	N/A	N/A	N/A	By Vehicle	500-600KG	1
285	N/A	1	N/A	N/A	N/A	By Foot	15KG	1
286	6:45PM	2	16	N/A	N/A	By Foot	5-6KG Each	2
287	N/A	1	N/A	N/A	N/A	By Vehicle	1200KG	1
288	8:40AM	3	N/A	Kalashinkov	N/A	By Foot	10-12KG	2
289	1:40PM	1	15	N/A	N/A	By Foot	N/A	1
290	8:10PM	1	N/A	Firing Handgrenade	N/A	By Vehicle	1000KG	2
291	N/A	1	N/A	N/A	N/A	By Foot	N/A	2
292	N/A	1	N/A	N/A	N/A	By Foot	N/A	1
293	8:45AM	1	17	N/A		By Foot	10-12KG	1
294	2:00PM First Blast	2	N/A	N/A	N/A	By Foot	N/A	2
295	11:15AM	1	N/A	N/A	N/A	By Foot	N/A	1
296	1:00PM	1	15	N/A	N/A	By Foot	10KG	1
297	4:00PM	1	N/A	N/A	N/A	By Vehicle	400KG	1
298	N/A	1	N/A	N/A	N/A	By Foot	10KG	1
299	N/A	1	N/A	N/A	N/A	By Foot	N/A	1
300	8:00AM	1	19	Hand Grenade	N/A	By Foot	N/A	2
301	N/A	1	N/A	N/A	N/A	By Foot	N/A	1
302	N/A	1	N/A	Hand Grenade	N/A	By Vehicle	1000KG	2
303	5:30PM	1	15	N/A	N/A	By Foot	4KG	1
304	N/A	1	N/A	N/A	N/A	N/A	N/A	1
305	N/A	1	N/A	N/A	N/A	By Foot	N/A	1
306	N/A	1	N/A	N/A	N/A	By Foot	7KG	1
307	8:15AM	1	17	N/A	N/A	By Foot	8-9KG	1
308	N/A	1	N/A	N/A	N/A	By Foot	N/A	1

309	N/A	1	N/A	N/A	N/A	By Vehicle	N/A	1
310	N/A	1	N/A	N/A	N/A	By Vehicle	400KG 250-300KG	1
311	N/A	1	19	N/A	N/A	By Foot	15-16KG 6-8KG	1
312	8:00AM	1	N/A	N/A	N/A	By Vehicle	200-250KG	1
313	11AM	1	N/A	N/A	N/A	By Foot	N/A	1
314	N/A	1	N/A	N/A	N/A	By Foot	N/A	1
315	N/A	1	15	N/A	N/A	By Foot	N/A	1
316	5:16PM	3	N/A	N/A	N/A	By Foot	N/A	2
317	N/A	1	15	N/A	N/A	By Foot	N/A	1
318	7:50AM	1	24	N/A	N/A	By Vehicle	180KG	1
319	N/A	1	N/A	N/A	N/A	By Foot	N/A	1
320	6:00AM	2	N/A	N/A	N/A	By Motor Bike	16-20KG	2
321	11:00AM	5	N/A	N/A	N/A	By Foot	N/A	1
322	4:30AM	1	N/A	Mortar Shells & MB12 Rockets	N/A	By Vehicle	300KG	1
323	N/A	1	N/A	N/A	N/A	By Vehicle	400-450KG	1
324	10:00AM	1	N/A	N/A	N/A	By Foot	N/A	1
325	8:45PM	1	N/A	N/A	N/A	By Foot	7-8KG	1
326	N/A	1	N/A	N/A	N/A	By Foot	8KG	3
327	2:00PM	1	18	N/A	Pashtoon	By Foot	N/A	1
328	N/A	2	N/A	Rifles	N/A	By Foot	N/A	2
329	N/A	1	20	N/A	N/A	By Foot	N/A	1
330	N/A	1	N/A	N/A	N/A	By Foot	N/A	1
331	N/A	1	Late Teens	N/A	N/A	By Foot	N/A	1
332	N/A	1	N/A	N/A	N/A	N/A	N/A	1
333	N/A	1	N/A	N/A	N/A	N/A	N/A	1
334	N/A	1	N/A	N/A	N/A	N/A	N/A	1
335	N/A	1	N/A	N/A	N/A	By Vehicle	N/A	1
336	N/A	1	N/A	N/A	N/A	By Vehicle	N/A	1
337	N/A	2	21	Firing	Afghan Refugee	By Vehicle / By Foot	100KG-15-20KG	2

338	N/A	1	N/A	N/A	N/A	By Foot	N/A	1
339	N/A	1	N/A	N/A	N/A	N/A	N/A	1
340	N/A	1	N/A	N/A	N/A	By Foot	N/A	1
341	N/A	1	N/A	N/A	N/A	N/A	N/A	1
342	N/A	5	N/A	N/A	N/A	By Vehicle	N/A	1
343	N/A	1	N/A	N/A	N/A	N/A	N/A	1
344	N/A	1	N/A	N/A	N/A	By Vehicle	N/A	1
345	N/A	1	N/A	N/A	N/A	N/A	N/A	1
346	1:00PM	2	N/A	N/A	N/A	N/A	N/A	1
347	2:00PM	4	N/A	Hand Grenade Rockets & Firing	N/A	By Foot	N/A	3
348	N/A	1	N/A	N/A	N/A	N/A	N/A	1
349	4:00PM	1	19	N/A	N/A	By Foot	3KG	1
350	N/A	1	N/A	N/A	N/A	By Foot	N/A	1
351	N/A	1	N/A	N/A	N/A	N/A	N/A	1
352	N/A	3	N/A	N/A	N/A	N/A	N/A	3
353	N/A	1	N/A	N/A	N/A	By Foot	N/A	1
354	N/A	1	22	N/A	N/A	By Foot	6KG	1
355	N/A	1	N/A	N/A	N/A	By Foot	N/A	1
356	N/A	1	N/A	N/A	N/A	By Foot	6KG	1
357	N/A	1	N/A	N/A	N/A	By Foot	6KG	1
358	N/A	1	N/A	N/A	N/A	By Foot	N/A	1
359	N/A	1	N/A	N/A	N/A	N/A	N/A	1
360	7:45AM	1	17	N/A	N/A	By Foot	N/A	1
361	N/A	1	N/A	N/A	N/A	By Vehicle	N/A	1
362	N/A	1	N/A	N/A	N/A	By Foot	N/A	1
363	N/A	N/A	N/A	N/A	N/A	By Vehicle	N/A	1
364	N/A	1	N/A	N/A	N/A	By Vehicle	30-50KG	1
365	9:30AM	2	N/A	Hand Grenade	N/A	By Vehicle	N/A	1
366	N/A	1	N/A	N/A	N/A	By Vehicle	N/A	1
367	N/A	9	N/A	N/A	N/A	N/A	N/A	N/A
368	N/A	1	N/A	N/A	N/A	By Vehicle	N/A	1
369	N/A	1	N/A	MB12 Rockets	N/A	By Vehicle	100-110KG	1
370	2:40PM	1	N/A	Mortars	N/A	By Vehicle	40KG	1
371	10:35AM	1	N/A	N/A	N/A	By Vehicle	30KG	1

372	2:30PM	1	22	N/A	N/A	By Vehicle	N/A	1
373	N/A	1	N/A	N/A	N/A	By Foot	7-8KG	1
374	6:55AM	1	N/A	N/A	N/A	By Vehicle	100-150KG	1
375	N/A	1	N/A	N/A	N/A	By Foot	N/A	1
376	N/A	1	N/A	N/A	N/A	By Foot	N/A	1
377	N/A	1	N/A	N/A	N/A	By Foot	12KG	1
378	N/A	1	14	N/A	N/A	By Motor Bike	N/A	1
379	N/A	1	N/A	N/A	N/A	By Vehicle	600-800KG	1
380	6:30AM	2	N/A	N/A	N/A	By Vehicle	N/A	1
381	N/A	3	N/A	Handgrenade & Firing	N/A	By Foot	N/A	3
382	N/A	1	N/A	N/A	N/A	By Foot	N/A	1
383	N/A	N/A	N/A	N/A	N/A	N/A	N/A	N/A
384	N/A	2	N/A	N/A	N/A	By Foot & By Vehicle	N/A	2
385	N/A	1	N/A	N/A	N/A	By Foot	6KG	1
386	5:00AM	1	N/A	N/A	N/A	N/A	N/A	1
387	N/A		N/A	N/A	N/A	N/A	N/A	
388	N/A	1	N/A	N/A	N/A	By Vehicle	N/A	1
389	N/A	5	N/A	N/A	N/A	N/A	N/A	5
390	N/A	N/A	N/A	N/A	N/A	N/A	N/A	1
391	6:00PM	1	N/A	N/A	N/A	By Vehicle	800KG	1
392	N/A	1	N/A	N/A	N/A	N/A	N/A	1
393	N/A	N/A	N/A	N/A	N/A	N/A	N/A	1
394	N/A	N/A	N/A	N/A	N/A	N/A	N/A	1
395	N/A	2	N/A	Handgrenade	N/A	By Foot	6KG	1
396	N/A	2	N/A	N/A	N/A	N/A	N/A	2
397	N/A	1	N/A	N/A	N/A	By Vehicle	N/A	1
398	N/A	1	N/A	N/A	N/A	By Foot	N/A	1
399	N/A	1	N/A	N/A	N/A	By Foot	N/A	1
400	N/A	1	N/A	N/A	N/A	N/A	N/A	1
401	N/A	1	N/A	N/A	N/A	N/A	N/A	1
402	N/A	1	N/A	N/A	N/A	N/A	N/A	1
403	N/A	1	N/A	N/A	N/A	N/A	N/A	1
404	N/A	1	N/A	N/A	N/A	N/A	N/A	1

405	N/A	1	N/A	N/A	N/A	N/A	N/A	1
406	N/A	1	N/A	N/A	N/A	By Foot	6KG	1
407	N/A	1	N/A	N/A	N/A	N/A	N/A	1
408	N/A	1	N/A	N/A	N/A	By Foot	N/A	1
409	N/A	1	N/A	N/A	N/A	By Vehicle	90-100KG	1
410	N/A	1	N/A	N/A	N/A	N/A	N/A	1
411	N/A	1	N/A	N/A	N/A	N/A	N/A	1
412	N/A	1	N/A	N/A	N/A	N/A	N/A	1
413	N/A	1	N/A	N/A	N/A	N/A	N/A	1
414	N/A	1	N/A	N/A	N/A	By Motorcycle	N/A	1
415	N/A	1	N/A	N/A	N/A	N/A	N/A	1
416	N/A	1	N/A	N/A	N/A	N/A	N/A	1
417	N/A	1	N/A	N/A	N/A	By Motorcycle	1000KG	1
418	N/A	1	N/A	N/A	N/A	N/A	N/A	1
419	N/A	1	N/A	N/A	N/A	By Foot	N/A	1
420	N/A	1	N/A	N/A	N/A	N/A	N/A	1
421	N/A	1	N/A	N/A	N/A	N/A	N/A	1
422	N/A	1	N/A	N/A	N/A	N/A	N/A	1
423	N/A	1	N/A	N/A	N/A	N/A	N/A	1
424	N/A	1	N/A	N/A	N/A	N/A	N/A	1
425	N/A	1	N/A	N/A	N/A	N/A	N/A	1
426	N/A	1	N/A	N/A	N/A	By Foot	N/A	1
427	N/A	1	N/A	Firing	N/A	By Foot	N/A	1
428	N/A	3	N/A	N/A	N/A	By Foot	6-7KG	1
429	N/A	1	N/A	N/A	N/A	N/A	N/A	1
430	N/A	1	N/A	N/A	N/A	N/A	N/A	1
431	N/A	1	N/A	N/A	N/A	By Bycycle	N/A	1
432	N/A	1	N/A	N/A	N/A	By Vehicle	N/A	1
433	N/A	1	N/A	N/A	N/A	By Foot	N/A	1
434	N/A	1	N/A	N/A	N/A	By Motorcycle	N/A	1
435	N/A	1	N/A	N/A	N/A	N/A	N/A	1
436	N/A	5	N/A	N/A	N/A	By Vehicle / By Foot	N/A	2
437	N/A	2	N/A	N/A	N/A	By Motorc/ By Foot	N/A	2

438	N/A	1	N/A	N/A	N/A	By Foot	N/A	1
439	N/A	1	N/A	N/A	N/A	N/A	N/A	1
440	N/A	1	N/A	N/A	N/A	N/A	N/A	1
441	N/A	2	21	Hand Grenade, Guns	Uzbek, Pashtun	By Foot	30kg	2
442	N/A	1	N/A	N/A	N/A	By Vehicle	N/A	1
443	N/A	1	N/A	N/A	N/A	N/A	N/A	1
444	N/A	1	N/A	N/A	N/A	By Vehicle	200KG	1
445	N/A	1	N/A	N/A	N/A	By Vehicle	N/A	1
446	N/A	1	N/A	N/A	N/A	By Vehicle	N/A	1
447	N/A	1	N/A	N/A	N/A	By Foot	N/A	1
448	N/A	1	N/A	N/A	N/A	N/A	N/A	1
449	N/A	1	N/A	N/A	N/A	By Vehicle	N/A	1
450	N/A	1	N/A	N/A	N/A	N/A	N/A	1
451	N/A	1	N/A	N/A	N/A	N/A	N/A	1
452	N/A	1	N/A	N/A	N/A	N/A	N/A	1
453	N/A	1	N/A	N/A	N/A	By Foot	N/A	1
454	N/A	1	N/A	N/A	N/A	N/A	N/A	1
455	N/A	1	N/A	N/A	N/A	By Vehicle	N/A	1
456	N/A	1	N/A	N/A	N/A	By Foot	N/A	1
457	N/A	1	N/A	N/A	N/A	By Vehicle	N/A	1
458	N/A	1	N/A	N/A	N/A		N/A	1
459	7:40AM	1	N/A	N/A	N/A	By Foot	N/A	1
460	N/A	1	N/A	N/A	N/A	N/A	N/A	1
461	N/A	1	24	N/A	N/A	By Foot	N/A	1
462	N/A	1	N/A	N/A	N/A	By Foot	N/A	1
463	N/A	1	N/A	N/A	N/A	N/A	N/A	1
464	N/A	3	N/A	N/A	N/A	By Foot	N/A	1
465	N/A	1	N/A	N/A	N/A	N/A	N/A	1
466	N/A	1	20	N/A	N/A	By Foot	6KG	1
467	N/A	1	N/A	N/A	N/A	By Foot	5KG	1
468	N/A	2	N/A	Firing With Different Weapons	N/A	By Foot	N/A	2
469	N/A	1	N/A	N/A	N/A	By Foot	N/A	1
470	N/A	1	N/A	N/A	N/A	By Foot	N/A	1
471	N/A	1	N/A	N/A	N/A	By Foot	8-10KG	1

472	9:20AM	1	N/A	N/A	N/A	N/A	N/A	1
473	N/A	10	N/A	Handgrenade/ Lunchers/ Automatic Weapons	Uzbek	By Foot	N/A	N/A
474	N/A	N/A	N/A	N/A	N/A	N/A	N/A	N/A
475	N/A	1	N/A	N/A	N/A	By Vehicle	N/A	1
476	N/A	1	N/A	N/A	N/A	By Vehicle	45 KG	1
477	N/A	1	N/A	N/A	N/A	By Foot	5-7 KG	1
478	N/A	1	N/A	N/A	N/A	By Foot	N/A	1
479	N/A	1	N/A	N/A	N/A	By Foot	6-8KG	1
480	N/A	1	N/A	N/A	N/A	By Foot	N/A	1
481	N/A	7	N/A	Automatic Weapons	N/A	By Foot	N/A	7
482	N/A	2	N/A	N/A	N/A	Explosion during search operation	N/A	
483	N/A	1	N/A	N/A	N/A	By Foot	6KG	1
484	N/A	5	N/A	Handgrenade & Firing	N/A	By Foot	N/A	1
485	N/A	1	N/A	N/A	N/A	By Foot	N/A	1
486	N/A	1	N/A	N/A	N/A	By Foot	N/A	1
487	N/A	2	N/A	Firing	N/A	By Foot	N/A	2
488	N/A	1	N/A	N/A	N/A	By Motorbike	6-7KG	1

					Claim		
No.	Foriegn.	Primary Target	Sect	Rel	Who	Statement	Speaker
1	4	Diplomates	N	N	Al-Gamma Al-Islamiya or Party of Islam	N/A	N/A
2	N/A	Journalists	N	N	N/A	N/A	N/A
3	11	Foreigners	N	N	Al-Qaeda or Indian involvement	N/A	N/A
4	N/A	Diplomates	N	N	N/A	N/A	N/A

5	N/A	Shia Community	Y	N	Lashkar-e-Jhangvi	N/A	N/A
6	N/A	Government	Y	N	N/A	N/A	N/A
7	N/A	President Pervez Musharraf	N	N	N/A	N/A	N/A
8	N/A	Shia Community	Y	N	N/A	N/A	N/A
9	N/A	Shia Community	Y	N	N/A	N/A	N/A
10	N/A	Shia Community	Y	N	N/A	N/A	N/A
11	N/A	Finance Minister	N	N	N/A	N/A	N/A
12	N/A	Shia Community	Y	N	N/A	N/A	N/A
13	N/A	Shia Community	Y	N	N/A	N/A	N/A
14	N/A	Shia Community	Y	N	N/A	N/A	N/A
15	N/A	No one	N	N	N/A	N/A	N/A
16	N/A	Shia Community	Y	N	N/A	N/A	N/A
17	N/A	Shia Community	Y	N	N/A	N/A	N/A
18	N/A	Shia Community	Y	N	N/A	N/A	N/A
19	N/A	Shia Community	Y	N	N/A	N/A	N/A
20	1	US Diplomat	N	N	N/A	N/A	N/A
21	N/A	Religious Political Party	N	N	N/A	N/A	N/A
22	N/A	Army	N	N	N/A	N/A	N/A
23	N/A	Security Forces	N	N	N/A	N/A	N/A
24	N/A	N/A	N	N	N/A	N/A	N/A
25	N/A	Army	N	N	N/A	N/A	N/A
26	N/A	Police	N	N	N/A	N/A	N/A
27	N/A	N/A	N	N	N/A	N/A	N/A

28	0		N	N	N/A	N/A	N/A
29	0	Army	N	N	N/A	N/A	N/A
30	0		N	N	N/A	N/A	N/A
31	0	Police	N	N	N/A	N/A	N/A
32	0		N	N	N/A	N/A	N/A
33	0		N	N	N/A	N/A	N/A
34	0	Soldiers	N	N	N/A	N/A	N/A
35	0		N	N	N/A	N/A	N/A
36	0		N	N	N/A	N/A	N/A
37	0	Soldiers	N	N	N/A	N/A	N/A
38	0	Government	N	N	N/A	N/A	N/A
39							
40	0		N	N	N/A	N/A	N/A
41	0	Soldiers	N	N	N/A	N/A	N/A
42	0	Political Agent	N	N	N/A	N/A	N/A
43	0	Soldiers	N	N	N/A	N/A	N/A
44	0	Soldiers	N	N	N/A	N/A	N/A
45	0	Police	N	N	N/A	N/A	N/A
46	0	Soldiers	N	N	N/A	N/A	N/A
47	0	Lawyers Convention	N	N	N/A	N/A	N/A
48	o	Soldiers	N	N	N/A	N/A	N/A
49	0	Chinese Engineers	N	N	N/A	N/A	N/A
50	0	Police	N	N	N/A	N/A	N/A
51	0	Soldiers	N	N	N/A	N/A	N/A
52	0	N/A	N	N	N/A	N/A	N/A
53	0	N/A	N	N	N/A	N/A	N/A
54	0	N/A	N	N	N/A	N/A	N/A
55	0	N/A	N	N	N/A	N/A	N/A
56	0	Soldiers	N	N	N/A	N/A	N/A
57	0	N/A	N	N	N/A	N/A	N/A
58	0	N/A	N	N	N/A	N/A	N/A
59	0	N/A	N	N	N/A	N/A	N/A
60	0	N/A	N	N	N/A	N/A	N/A
61	0	Soldiers	N	N	N/A	N/A	N/A

62	0	Soldiers	N	N	N/A	N/A	N/A
63	0	Police	N	N	N/A	N/A	N/A
64		Soldiers	N	N	N/A	N/A	N/A
65	0	Soldiers	N	N	N/A	N/A	N/A
66	0	N/A	N	N	N/A	N/A	N/A
67	0	N/A	N	N	N/A	N/A	N/A
68	0	N/A	N	N	N/A	N/A	N/A
69	0	Soldiers	N	N	N/A	N/A	N/A
70	0	Soldiers	N	N	N/A	N/A	N/A
71	0	N/A	N	N	N/A	N/A	N/A
72	0	Benazir Bhutto	N	N	N/A	N/A	N/A
73	0	FC	N	N	N/A	N/A	N/A
74	0	Government	N	N	N/A	N/A	N/A
75	0	Pakistan Air Force	N	N	N/A	N/A	N/A
76	0	Government	N	N	N/A	N/A	N/A
77	0	Government	N	N	N/A	N/A	N/A
78	o	Army	N	N	N/A	N/A	N/A
79	0	N/A	N	N	N/A	N/A	N/A
80	0	N/A	N	N	N/A	N/A	N/A
81	0	N/A	N	N	N/A	N/A	N/A
82	0	Army	N	N	N/A	N/A	N/A
83	0	Army	N	N	N/A	N/A	N/A
84	0	Army	N	N	N/A	N/A	N/A
85	0	N/A	N	N	N/A	N/A	N/A
86	0	FC	N	N	N/A	N/A	N/A
87	0	Ex Prime Minister	N	N	N/A	N/A	N/A
88	0	N/A	N	N	N/A	N/A	N/A
89	0	Police	N	N	N/A	N/A	N/A
90	0	Security Forces	N	N	N/A	N/A	N/A
91	0	N/A	Y	N	N/A	N/A	N/A
92							
93	0	Security Forces	N	N	N/A	N/A	N/A
94	0	Army	N	N	N/A	N/A	N/A

95	0	N/A	N	N	N/A	N/A	N/A
96	0	Political Gathering	N	N	N/A	N/A	N/A
97	0	Political Gathering	N	N	N/A	N/A	N/A
98	0	Army	N	N	N/A	N/A	N/A
99	0	Political Gathering	N	N	N/A	N/A	N/A
100	0	Army	N	N	N/A	N/A	N/A
101	0	N/A	N	N	N/A	N/A	N/A
102	0	Security Forces	N	N	N/A	N/A	N/A
103	0	Tribel Jirga	N	N	N/A	N/A	N/A
104	0	Navy	N	N	N/A	N/A	N/A
105	0	Security Agency	N	N	N/A	N/A	N/A
106	0	N/A	N	N	N/A	N/A	N/A
107	0	Police	N	N	N/A	N/A	N/A
108	0	Army	N	N	Mulvi Nazir Group	N/A	Commander Malang
109	0	N\A	N	N	N/A	N/A	N/A
110	0	Security Forces	N	N	N/A	N/A	N/A
111	0	Police	N	N	N/A	N/A	N/A
112	0	Army	N	N	Local Taliban	N/A	N/A
113	0	Danish Embassy	N	N	N/A	N/A	N/A
114	0	N\A	N	N	N/A	N/A	N/A
115	0	N/A	Y	N	N/A	N/A	N/A
116	0	Police	N	N	N/A	N/A	N/A
117	0	N/A	Y	N	TTP	N/A	Mulvi Omar
118	0	Ordnance Factory	N	N	TTP	N/A	Mulvi Omar
119	0	N/A	N	N	N/A	N/A	N/A
120	0	Police	N	N	TTP	N/A	Muslim khan
121	0	Security Forces	N	N	TTP	N/A	Mohammad

122	0	N/A	N	N	TTP	N/A	N/A
123	0	Security Forces	N	N	N/A	N/A	N/A
124	0	School Children/ Police	N	N	N/A	N/A	N/A
125	0	N/A	N	N	N/A	N/A	N/A
126	0	Army	N	N	N/A	N/A	N/A
127	0	Army	N	N	N/A	N/A	N/A
128	0	N/A	N	N	N/A	N/A	N/A
129	0	Police	N	N	N/A	N/A	N/A
130	0	Politician	N	N	N/A	N/A	N/A
131	0	N/A	N	N	N/A	N/A	N/A
132	0	Police	N	N	N/A	N/A	N/A
133	0	NATO Supply	N	N	N/A	N/A	N/A
134	0	Tribel Jirga	N	N	N/A	N/A	N/A
135	0	Police	N	N	N/A	N/A	N/A
136	0	Security Forces	N	N	N/A	N/A	N/A
137	0	Army	N	N	N/A	N/A	N/A
138	0	Police	N	N	N/A	N/A	N/A
139	0	Security Forces	N	N	N/A	N/A	N/A
140	0	Security Forces	N	N	N/A	N/A	N/A
141	0	Tribel Jirga	N	N	N/A	N/A	N/A
142	0	Police	N	N	N/A	N/A	N/A
143	0	N/A	N	N	N/A	N/A	N/A
144	0	Security Forces	N	N	N/A	N/A	N/A
145	0	Security Forces	N	N	TTP Swat	N/A	Muslim khan
146	0	N/A	N	N	N/A	N/A	N/A
147	0	Police	N	N	N/A	N/A	N/A
148	0	N/A	N	N	N/A	N/A	N/A
149	0	N/A	N	N	N/A	N/A	N/A
150	0	N/A	N	N	N/A	N/A	N/A

151	0	N/A	N	N	N/A	N/A	N/A
152	0	N/A	N	N	TTP	N/A	Muslim khan
153	0	Police	N	N	N/A	N/A	N/A
154	0	Police	N	N	N/A	N/A	N/A
155	0	Security Forces	N	N	N/A	N/A	N/A
156	0	Police	N	N	N/A	N/A	N/A
157	0	Religious Gathering	Y	N	N/A	N/A	N/A
158	0	NATO Supply	N	N	TTP	Taliban Spokesman Claimed Responsibility For The Attack And Threatened More Attacks On The NATO Supply Route Unless The Government Halted Military Operations In The Agency	N/A
159	0	Security Forces	N	N	N/A	N/A	N/A
160	0		Y	N	N/A	N/A	N/A
161	0	Police	N	N	N/A	N/A	N/A
162	0	Police	N	N	N/A	N/A	N/A
163	0	N/A	N	N	N/A	N/A	N/A
164	0	Politician	N	N	N/A	N/A	N/A
165	0	N/A	N	N	N/A	N/A	N/A
166	0	Police	N	N	N/A	N/A	N/A
167	0	Peace Committee	N	N	TTP	N/A	Mulvi Omar
168	0	N/A	N	N	N/A	N/A	N/A
169	0	N/A	N	N	N/A	N/A	N/A
170	0	Police	N	N	N/A	N/A	N/A
171	0	Security Forces	N	N	N/A	N/A	N/A
172	0	Security Forces	N	N	N/A	N/A	N/A
173	0	Imambargah	Y	N	N/A	N/A	N/A
174	0	Police	N	N	N/A	N/A	N/A

175	0	Security Forces	N	N	TTP	The Drones Should Be Stopped And Withdrawal Of Troops	N/A
176	0	Security Forces	N	N	N/A	N/A	N/A
177	0	Security Forces	N	N	N/A	N/A	N/A
178	0	Security Forces	N	N	N/A	N/A	N/A
179	0	Police	N	N	N/A	N/A	N/A
180	0	Security Forces	N	N	N/A	N/A	N/A
181	0	Police	N	N	N/A	N/A	N/A
182	0	N/A	N	N	N/A	N/A	N/A
183	0	Police	N	N	N/A	N/A	N/A
184	3	N/A	N	N	N/A	N/A	N/A
185	0	Security Forces	N	N	N/A	N/A	N/A
186	0	Anti Taliban Cleric	N	N	N/A	N/A	N/A
187	0	Security Forces	N	N	N/A	N/A	N/A
188	0	Police	N	N	N/A	N/A	N/A
189	0	Security Forces	N	N	TTP		Hakimullah Mehsud
190	0	N/A	N	N	N/A	N/A	N/A
191	0	NATO Supply	N	N	N/A	N/A	N/A
192	0	Police	N	N	N/A	N/A	N/A
193	0	Kahuta Research Laboratories	N	N	N/A	N/A	N/A
194	0	N/A	N	N	N/A	N/A	N/A
195	0	Security Forces	N	N	Local Taliban	N/A	N/A
196	0	Pro Goverment Tribal Leader	N	N	N/A	N/A	N/A

197	0	Security Forces	N	N	N/A	N/A	N/A
198	0	Security Forces	N	N	N/A	N/A	N/A
199	0	Security Forces	N	N	N/A	N/A	N/A
200	0	N/A	N	N	N/A	N/A	N/A
201	0	Security Forces	N	N	Abdullah Azzam Brigade	N/A	N/A
202	0	Police	N	N	N/A	N/A	N/A
203	0	Police	N	N	N/A	N/A	N/A
204	0	Security Forces	N	N	N/A	N/A	N/A
205	0	Security Forces	N	N	N/A	N/A	N/A
206	0	N/A	Y	N	Lashkar e Jhangvi Al Almi	It is Said To Be The Revenge Of Religious Leader And Warned Of More Attacks In Future	Mulana Rauf
207	0	Security Forces	N	N	N/A	N/A	N/A
208	0	Police, Education Minister	N	N	N/A	N/A	N/A
209	0	N/A	N	N	N/A	N/A	N/A
210	0	Police	N	N	TTP	N/A	Qari Hussain
211	0	Pro Goverment Cleric	N	N	N/A	N/A	N/A
212	1	UN Officials	N	N	N/A	N/A	N/A
213	0	N/A	N	N	N/A	N/A	N/A
214	0	Military Convoy	N	N	N/A	N/A	N/A
215	0	Police Station	N	N	TTP	Taliban Warned To Attack Three Sensitive Installations In Kohat	Usman Ali

216	0	Forces Training Centre	N	N	N/A	N/A	N/A
217	0	Security Agency	N	N	N/A	N/A	N/A
218	0	N/A	N	N	N/A	N/A	N/A
219	0	Pakistan Aeronauticals Complex	N	N	N/A	N/A	N/A
220	0	N/A	N	N	N/A	N/A	N/A
221	0	N/A	N	N	N/A	N/A	N/A
222	0	N/A	N	N	N/A	N/A	N/A
223	0	Head Of Peace Lashkar	N	N	TTP	If Anybody Else Dares To Raise A Lashkar (militia) Against Us He Will Be Dealt With In Same Manner	Azam Tariq
224	0	N/A	N	N	N/A	N/A	N/A
225	0	N/A	N	N	N/A	N/A	N/A
226	0	Secret Agency	N	N	N/A	N/A	N/A
227	0	Police	N	N	N/A	N/A	N/A
228	0	N/A	N	N	N/A	N/A	N/A
229	0	Police	N	N	N/A	N/A	N/A
230	0	N/A	N	N	N/A	N/A	N/A
231	0	Member Provincial Assembly	N	N	N/A	N/A	N/A
232	0	Naval Headquarters	N	N	N/A	N/A	N/A
233	0	Army	N	N	TTP	N/A	Ameer Wali ur Rehman
234	0	N/A	N	N	N/A	N/A	N/A
235	0	N/A	N	N	N/A	N/A	N/A
236	0	Secret Agency	N	N	N/A	N/A	N/A
237	0	N/A	N	N	N/A	N/A	N/A
238	0	N/A	N	N	N/A	N/A	N/A
239	0	N/A	N	N	N/A	N/A	N/A

240	0	Journalists	N	N	N/A	N/A	N/A
241	0	N/A	N	N	N/A	N/A	N/A
242	0	Muharram Procession	Y	N	N/A	N/A	N/A
243	0	Muharram Procession	Y	N	N/A	N/A	N/A
244	0	Muharram Procession	Y	N	N/A	N/A	N/A
245	0	N/A	N	N	N/A	N/A	N/A
246	0	Army	N	N	N/A	N/A	N/A
247	0	Militant outfit Ansar-ul Islam	N	N	N/A	N/A	N/A
248	0	Police	N	N	N/A	N/A	N/A
249	0	Security Forces	N	N	N/A	N/A	N/A
250	0	Police	N	N	N/A	N/A	N/A
251	0	N/A	N	N	N/A	N/A	N/A
252	0	Security Forces	N	N	N/A	N/A	N/A
253	0	Police	N	N	N/A	N/A	N/A
254	0	N/A	N	N	N/A	N/A	N/A
255	0	Police	N	N	TTP Janud Ul Hifsa Group	N/A	Abdullah Ghazi
256	1	Security Forces	N	N	N/A	N/A	N/A
257	0	Police	N	N	TTP	Both Police And Army Are Our Enemies We Will Carry Out More Attacks Police	Azam Tariq
258	0	Convoy Carrying Shia	Y	N	N/A	N/A	N/A
259	0	Investigation Unit	N	N	TTP	N/A	Azam Tariq
260	0	Paramilitary Convoy	N	N	N/A	N/A	N/A
261	0	N/A	N	N	N/A	N/A	N/A

262	0	N/A	N	N	TTP	N/A	Azam Tariq
263	0	Anti Taliban Tribal Leader	N	N	N/A	N/A	N/A
264	0	N/A	N	N	N/A	N/A	N/A
265	3	US Consulate	N	N	TTP	Attack Was Reaction To Military Operations And Drones Attacks In Tribel Area	Azam Tariq
266	0	Political Gathering	N	N	N/A	N/A	N/A
267	0	Shia Community	Y	N	Lashkar e Jhangvi	N/A	Ali Sher Haidri
268	0	Shia Community	Y	N	Lashkar e Jhangvi Al Almi	N/A	N/A
269	0	Police	N	N	TTP	N/A	Qari Hussain
270	0	N/A	N	N	N/A	N/A	N/A
271	0	N/A	N	N	TTP	N/A	Azam Tariq
272	0	N/A	N	N	N/A	N/A	N/A
273	0	Ahmadis Community	N	Y	TT Punjab Wing	N/A	N/A
274	0	Religious Gathering	N	N	N/A	N/A	N/A
275	0	Political Agent And Jirga Against Taliban	N	N	TTP Mohmand	That Their Targets Were Offices Of The Political Administration And Local Peace Committee Which Had Arranged An Anti Taliban Jirga There We Have No Enmity With The People He Added	Ikramullah
276	0	Tribal Elder in Fata	N	N	N/A	N/A	N/A
277	0	Shia Community	Y	N	N/A	N/A	N/A

278	0	Goverment Minister	N	N	TTP	Our Goal Was To Kill Mian Iftekhar Hussain Because His Political Party Is Allied With United States This Is Just The Begining	Ahsanullah Ahsan
279	0	F.C Commandant	N	N	TTP	We Killed Him He Was Our Target All Sach Officers Who Are Active Against Us Will Suffer The Same Fate	Azam Tariq
280	0	Pro Goverment Cleric	N	N	N/A	N/A	N/A
281	0	Shia Community	Y	N	Lashkar e Jhangvi Al Almi	N/A	N/A
282	0	Ahmadis Community	Y	Y	N/A	N/A	N/A
283	0	Shia Community	Y	N	Lashkar e Jhangvi	N/A	Ali Sher Haidri
284	0	Police	N	N	TTP	The Attack Was To Carried Out To Avenge The Killing Of Their Commander At The Hands Of Security Forces In Lakki A few days Back	Ehsanullah Ehsan
285	0	Goverment Minister	N	N	N/A	N/A	N/A
286	0	N/A	N	N	TTP	N/A	N/A
287	0	N/A	N	N	N/A	N/A	N/A
288	0	Police	N	N	TTP	We Will Continue To Target Police Security Forces Until Drone Attacks And Military Operations against Taliban Are Stopped	Azam Tariq

289	0	N/A	N	N	TTP	They Formed Lashkar Against Us Declared War Against Taliban	N/A
290	0	Investigation Agency	N	N	TTP	The Attack Was In Retalition For US Air Strikes In The Country North West Trible Area	Azam Tariq
291	0	Security Forces	N	N	N/A	N/A	N/A
292	0	Member of Shakai Peace Committee	N	N	N/A	N/A	N/A
293	0	Police	N	N	N/A	N/A	N/A
294	0	Peace Committee	N	N	TTP	Those Who Will Work Agianst Us And Form Lashkar (Tribal Army) Or Peace Committee Will Be Targeted. Our War Is To Enforce Sharia And Anyone Who Hinders Our Way Or Sides America Will Meet The Same Fate	Omar Khalid
295	0	Chief Minister	N	N	BULF	N/A	Shehk Baloch
296	0	N/A	N	N	TTP	N/A	Usman Ali
297	0	Shia Community	Y	N	Lashkar e Jhangvi Al Almi		Abu Bakar Mansoor
298	0	N/A	N	N	N/A	N/A	N/A
299	0	Shia Community	Y	N	N/A	N/A	N/A
300	0	Pro Goverment Tribe	N	N	TTP	The Attack Was Retaliation For The Salarzai Tribe's Activities Against The Taliban	Azam Tariq
301	0	Muharram Procession	Y	N	N/A	N/A	N/A

302	0	N/A	N	N	TTP	He Vowed To Carry Out More Such Attacks And Adding That The Goverment Was Following US Dictation	Ehsanullah Ehsan
303	0	Shia Community	Y	N	N/A	N/A	N/A
304	0	Shia Community	Y	N	N/A	N/A	N/A
305	0	Law Enforecement Personnel	N	N	N/A	N/A	N/A
306	0	Police	N	N	N/A	N/A	N/A
307	0	Army	N	N	TTP	N/A	Ehsanullah Ehsan
308	0	N/A	N	N	N/A	N/A	N/A
309	0	Police	N	N	N/A	N/A	N/A
310	0	N/A	N	N	N/A	N/A	N/A
311	0	Anti Taliban Militia Leader	N	N	TTP	N/A	Hamza
312	0	Police	N	N	N/A	N/A	N/A
313	0	Religious Party Leader	N	N	N/A	N/A	N/A
314	0	Religious Party Leader	N	N	N/A	N/A	N/A
315	0	N/A	N	N	N/A	N/A	N/A
316	0	N/A	N	N	N/A	N/A	N/A
317	0	Anti Taliban Tribal Leader	N	N	N/A	N/A	N/A
318	0	Police	N	N	N/A	N/A	N/A
319	0	Tribal Militia Chief	N	N	N/A	N/A	N/A
320	0	F.C	N	N	N/A	This Was The First Revenge For Osama's Martyrdom. Wait For Bigger Attacks In Pakistan And Aghanistan	Ehsanullah Ehsan
321	0	N/A	N	N	N/A	N/A	N/A

322	0	Investigation Agency	N	N	TTP	This Was For The Revenge Of Osama	N/A
323	0	Police	N	N	TTP	Soon You Will See Bigger Attacks. Revange For Osama Cant Be Satisfied Just With Small Attacks	Ehsanullah Ehsan
324	0	Anti Taliban Tribal Leader	N	N	TTP	The Elders Were Targeted Becouse They Were Helping The security Forces	Ehsanullah Ehsan
325	0	Army	N	N	N/A	N/A	N/A
326	0	N/A	N	N	N/A	N/A	N/A
327	0	N/A	N	N	N/A	N/A	N/A
328	0	Police	N	N	TTP	Saying It Was Partly In Revenge For The US Raid That Killed Al Qaeda Chief Osama Bin Laden	Ehsanullah Ehsan
329	0	Political Rally	N	N	N/A	N/A	N/A
330	0	Employees of Frontier Works Organisation	N	N	N/A	N/A	N/A
331	0	Security Forces	N	N	N/A	N/A	N/A
332	0	N/A	N	N	N/A	N/A	N/A
333	0	Police	N	N	N/A	N/A	N/A
334	0	Friday prayer	N	Y	N/A	N/A	N/A
335	0	Shia	Y	N	N/A	N/A	N/A
336	N/A	Security Forces	N	N	N/A	N/A	N/A
337	0	D.I.G F.C	N	N	TTP	To Avenge The Arrest Of Our Mujahideen Brothers By Pakistani Security Forces In Quetta Recently	Ehsanullah Ehsan
338	0	Funeral Participants	N	N	N/A	N/A	N/A

339	0	Police - Chaudhary Aslam (ssp CID)	N	N	N/A	N/A	N/A
340	0	Police - Ajmeer Shah (senior police anti-ttp official)	N	N	N/A	N/A	N/A
341	0	ANP Teshil Nazim - Hanif Jadoon	N	N	N/A	N/A	N/A
342	0	Police	N	N	N/A	N/A	N/A
343	0	N/A	N	N	N/A	N/A	N/A
344	0	FC	N	N	N/A	N/A	N/A
345	0	Tribal Elder in Balochistan - ShafiqMengal	N	N	N/A	N/A	N/A
346	0	N/A	N	N	N/A	N/A	N/A
347	0	Police	N	N	N/A	N/A	N/A
348	0	Police	N	N	N/A	N/A	N/A
349	0	Rivals Of Taliban	N	N	Lashkar e Islami	N/A	N/A
350	0	Pro Goverment Militia	N	N	N/A	N/A	N/A
351	0	Shia Community	Y	N	TTP	We Have Targeted Shia Community Of Parachinar Because They Were Involved In Activities Against Us	Fazal Saeed
352	0	Police	N	N	N/A	N/A	N/A
353	0	Friday prayer	N	Y	N/A	N/A	N/A
354	0	Political Leader	N	N	TTP	We Made This Attack Because Aftab Sherpao Has Cooperated With The Goverment For An Operation Against Us In The Tribal Areas.	Omar Khalid

355	0	Police	N	N	N/A	N/A	N/A
356	0	Deputy Speaker Of KPK Assembly	N	N	TTP	Deputy Speaker OF KPK Assembly Was Target Because He Was Assisting The Local Peace Committees In Combating The Militants	N/A
357	0	Police	N	N	N/A	N/A	N/A
358	0	Rivals Of Taliban	N	N	TTP Tariq Group	N/A	Mohammad
359	0	Police	N	N	N/A	N/A	N/A
360	0	Commander Of Security Forces	N	N	TTP	Rabi Was There main Target Adding That Lattar Was Involved In the Killing Of Senior Alqaeda Militant Sheikh Marwan.	Ahsanullah Ahsan
361	0	Goverment Employees	N	N	N/A	N/A	N/A
362	0	Peace Militia Chief	N	N	N/A	N/A	N/A
363	0	University Bus	N	N	N/A	N/A	N/A
364	0	Shia Zaireen	Y	N	Lashkar e Jhangvi	N/A	Abu Bakar
365	0	Police	N	N	TTP		Ehsanullah Ehsan
366	0	Pro Government militant - Maulvi Nabi	N	N	N/A	N/A	N/A
367	0	PAF	N	N	N/A	N/A	N/A
368	N/A	Security Forces	N	N	N/A	N/A	N/A
369	0	US Consulate Vehicle	N	N	N/A	N/A	N/A
370	0	N/A	N	N	N/A	N/A	N/A

371	0	Peace Militia Office	N	N	N/A	N/A	N/A
372	0	Peace Militia Leader	N	N	TTP	Fateh Khan Was Our Enemy No 1 He Had Killed A Number Of Our Colleagues In Buner	Ehsanullah Ehsan
373	0	Police	N	N	TTP	Alleging That The Slain Police Officer Was Targeted As He Resorted To Torture Of Taliban Suspects During Interrogation	Ehsanullah Ehsan
374	0	Security Forces	N	N	TTP	It Was The Revenge For The Arrest, Torture And Killing Of Our People By Security Forces	Sirajuddin Ahmed
375	0	A Religious Leader	N	N	N/A	N/A	N/A
376	0	Shia Community	Y	N	N/A	N/A	N/A
377	0	Shia Community	Y	N	TTP	That Taliban Had Dispatched More Suicide Bombers Across The Country For The Attacks Against The Minority Community	Ehsanullah Ehsan
378	0	Mullah Nazir Pro Goverment Taliban Commander	N	N	N/A	N/A	N/A
379	0	Police	N	N	TTP	The TTP Would Continue Attacks On Police As They Are The Main Hurdle In Our Way He Stressed	Ehsanullah Ehsan
380	0	Army	N	N	N/A	N/A	N/A
381	N/A	Security Forces	N	N	TTP	N/A	N/A
382	N/A	Minister	N	N	TTP	N/A	N/A

383	0	Tablighi Jamaat	N	Y	N/A	N/A	N/A
384	0	Shia Community	Y	N	Lashkar e Jhangvi	N/A	N/A
385	0	Shia Community	Y	N	N/A	N/A	N/A
386	0	Army	N	N	N/A	N/A	N/A
387	0	N/A			N/A	N/A	N/A
388	0	Police, Levies, FC	N	N	N/A	N/A	N/A
389	0	Police and Law Enforcement Agencies	N	N	N/A	N/A	N/A
390	0	N/A	N	N	N/A	N/A	N/A
391	0	Shia Community	Y	N	Lashkar e Jhangvi	N/A	N/A
392	0	Political Agent (Khyber Agency)	N	N	N/A	N/A	N/A
393	0	N/A	N	N	N/A	N/A	N/A
394	0	N/A	N	N	N/A	N/A	N/A
395	0	Courts	N	N	N/A	N/A	N/A
396	0	Militants (including an uzbek commander)	N	N	N/A	N/A	N/A
397	0	Security Forces	N	N	N/A	N/A	N/A
398	0	Security Forces	N	N	TTP	We Claim Responsibilty For The Attack Which Was Carried Out Against Those Who Guard A Secular System And Carry Out Operations In The Trible Area	Ehsanullah Ehsan
399	0	Police	N	N	N/A	N/A	N/A
400	0	N/A	N	N	N/A	N/A	N/A
401	0	N/A	N	N	N/A	N/A	N/A

402	0	N/A	N	N	N/A	N/A	N/A
403	0	N/A	N	N	N/A	N/A	N/A
404	0	N/A	N	N	N/A	N/A	N/A
405	0	Soldiers	N	N	N/A	N/A	N/A
406	0	Political Rally	N	N	N/A	N/A	N/A
407	0	N/A	N	N	N/A	N/A	N/A
408	0	N/A	N	N	N/A	N/A	N/A
409	0	Shia Community	Y	N	Lashkar e Jhangvi	N/A	N/A
410	0	N/A	N	N	N/A	N/A	N/A
411	0	Political Rally	N	N	N/A	N/A	N/A
412	0	Religious Party Rally	N	N	N/A	N/A	N/A
413	0	Political Rally	N	N	N/A	N/A	N/A
414	0	N/A	N	N	N/A	N/A	N/A
415	0	N/A	N	N	N/A	N/A	N/A
416	0	N/A	N	N	N/A	N/A	N/A
417	0	Police Chief	N	N	N/A	N/A	N/A
418	0	N/A	N	N	N/A	N/A	N/A
419	0	N/A	N	N	N/A	N/A	N/A
420	0	N/A	N	N	N/A	N/A	N/A
421	0	N/A	N	N	N/A	N/A	N/A
422	0	N/A	N	N	N/A	N/A	N/A
423	0	Shia Comunity	Y	N	N/A	N/A	N/A
424	0	N/A	N	N	N/A	N/A	N/A
425	0	Police	N	N	N/A	N/A	N/A
426	0	Shia Community	Y	N	Lashkar e Jhangvi	N/A	N/A
427	0	N/A	N	N	N/A	N/A	N/A
428	0	Shia Community	Y	N	N/A	N/A	N/A
429	0	N/A	N	N	N/A	N/A	N/A
430	0	Shia Community	Y	N	N/A	N/A	N/A

431	0	Shia Community	Y	N	N/A	N/A	N/A
432	0	Security Forces	N	N	N/A	N/A	N/A
433	0	Afghan Security Forces	N	N	N/A	N/A	N/A
434	0	Tribal Elder	N	N	N/A	N/A	N/A
435	0	Afghan Security Forces, FC	N	N	N/A	N/A	N/A
436	0	Secret Agency	N	N	TTP Janudullah Group	N/A	N/A
437	0	Shia Community	Y	N	N/A	N/A	N/A
438	0	Police	N	N	TTP	We Did It And Soon You Will See Another Big Attack We Are In War With Police and Security Agencies	Shahidullah Shahid
439	0	Police	N	N	N/A	N/A	N/A
440	0	Police	N	N	N/A	N/A	N/A
441	0	Christians	N	Y	Junduallah	We Will Continue Our Attacks On Non Muslims On Pakistani Land	Ahmed Marwat
442	0	Militants	N	N	N/A	N/A	N/A
443	0	N/A	N	N	N/A	N/A	N/A
444	0	Anti Taliban Group	N	N	TTP	Taliban Had Carried Out The Attack Because Molana Nabi Is Our Enemy And TTP Will Continue To Attack Him	Shahidullah Shahid
445	0	Anti Taliban Cleric	N	N	TTP	N/A	Shahidullah Shahid
446	0	Security Forces	N	N	N/A	N/A	N/A
447	0	Minister	N	N	N/A	N/A	N/A

448	N/A	Security Forces	N	N	N/A	N/A	N/A
449	N/A	Security Forces	N	N	N/A	N/A	N/A
450	0	N/A	N	N	N/A	N/A	N/A
451	0	N/A	N	N	N/A	N/A	N/A
452	0	N/A	N	N	N/A	N/A	N/A
453	0	Shia Community	Y	N	N/A	N/A	N/A
454	0	N/A	N	N	N/A	N/A	N/A
455	0	Shia Community	Y	N	Jaish Al Islam	The Bombing Was In Revenge For The Rawalpindi Attack An Alleged Incident Of Desecration Holy Quran In Quetta	Ghazi Haqnawaz
456	0	School	N	N	N/A	N/A	N/A
457	0	Police-Aslam Chadhry CID SP	N	N	TTP	N/A	N/A
458	0	Army	N	N	N/A	N/A	N/A
459	0	Army	N	N	TTP	N/A	N/A
460	0	N/A			N/A	N/A	N/A
461	0	Security Forces	N	N	N/A	N/A	N/A
462	0	N/A	N	N	N/A	N/A	N/A
463	0	Police and Intelligence Officials	N	N		N/A	N/A
464	0	N/A	N	N	N/A	N/A	N/A
465	0	Police	N	N	TTP	"We carried out the attack against the police because they are killing our people"	Shahidullah Shahid
466	0	Security Forces	N	N	N/A	N/A	N/A
467	0	Iranian Consulate	N	N	N/A	N/A	N/A
468	0	Courts	N	N	N/A	N/A	N/A
469	0	Police	N	N	N/A	N/A	N/A

470	0	Police	N	N	TTP	The Police Officer Have Killed Many Taliban In Fake Inco	N/A
471	0	IDPs	N	N	N/A	N/A	N/A
472	0	Army	N	N	TTP	They Attack Was Carried Out By TTP Attackers To Protect The Killing Of Seven TTP Activists In Karachi And Killing Taliban In Jail	Shahidullah Shahid
473	0	Airport	N	N	TTP		
474	0	Paramilitary Soldiers	N	N	N/A	N/A	N/A
475	0	N/A	N	N	N/A	N/A	N/A
476	0	Security Forces	N	N		The Attack Was Recation of Zarb_i_ azab Operation	Shahidullah Shahid
477	0	Shia Community	Y	N	N/A	N/A	N/A
478	0	Tribal Elders	N	N	N/A	N/A	N/A
479	0	A Religious Leader	N	N	Jundallah Group	N/A	N/A
480	0		N	N	Jundallah Group, TTP	N/A	N/A
481	N/A	School	N	N	TTP	N/A	N/A
482	0		N	N	N/A	N/A	N/A
483	N/A	Shia Community	Y	N	Jandullah Group	Our Target Was The Shia Mosque They Are Our Enemies	Fahad Marwat
484	N/A	Shia Community	Y	N	TTP	N/A	N/A
485	N/A	N/A	N	N	TTP Ahrar Group		Ehsan Ul Ehsan
486	N/A	Shia Community	Y	N	N/A	N/A	N/A
487	N/A	Christians	N	Y	N/A	N/A	N/A
488	N/A	Security Forces	N	N	N/A	N/A	N/A

No.	Occasion	Hospital Injured/ Dead Taken to	Note 1	Note 2
1	N/A	N/A	SOURCE: New straits times	
2	N/A	N/A	SOURCE: International Freedom of Expression Exchange	
3	N/A	Jinnah Postgraduate Medical Center(JPMC), Civil Hospital Karachi, PN Shifa and Agha Khan Hospital.	The French Tecnicians Were Part Of A Force Of 80 Working On A Joint Venture With Pakistan To Build Three Agosta 90B Class Submarines	
4	N/A	N/A		
5	Friday Prayers	Combined Military Hospital		
6	N/A	N/A	Failed attempt to kill Musharraf	
7	N/A	RGH and District Headquarters Hospital		
8	N/A	Local Hospital	The Bomber Died Only	
9	Friday Prayers	Civil Hospital		
10	N/A	Civil Hospital, Jinnah Postgraduate Medial Center, Liaquat National, Hospital.		
11	Election Compaign	Islamabad Hospitals, Tehsil Headquarters Hospitals, Fatehjang, PIMS, Headquarters Hospitals.	Finance Minister Shaukat Aziz Was Contesting By Election To Become Prime Minister	
12	Friday Prayers	Allama Iqbal Memorial DHQ Hospital, Sardar begum hospital		
13	N/A	Mayo Hospital		
14	Gathering At Shia Saint Shrine	N/A		
15	Bomb blew while it was being planted	N/A		

16	Urs of Bari Imam	Polyclinic Hospital, Capital Development Authourity (CDA) Hospital		
17	N/A	Liaquat National Hospital, Jinnah Postgraduate Medical Center, JPMC, Petal Hospital.		
18	Muharram Pocession			
19	Ashura	Hungo District Headquarters Hospital		
20	N/A	JPMC & PN Shifa		
21	Eid Miladun Nabi Procession	Civil Hospital Abbasi Shaheed Hospital & JPMC		
22	N/A	Combined Military Hospital bannu & Combined Military Hospital Peshawar		
23	N/A	N/A		
24	N/A	N/A		
25	N/A	Combined Military Hospital Rawalpindi & Combined Military Hospital Peshawar		
26	N/A	N/A		
27	N/A	N/A		
28	Republic Day of India's Function	N/A		
29	N/A	N/A		
30	Republic Day Function Hosted by India's High Commission	Polyclinic Hospital		
31	Arrangements For Procession	Lady Reading Hospital		
32	N/A	N/A		

33	N/A	N/A		
34	Soldiers: Dera Ismail Khan To Tank	N/A		
35	N/A	N/A	When a grenade that he had attempted to throw at the security guard landed near the militant's foot and exploded.	
36	N/A	Civil Hospital, BMC		
37	N/A	Combined Military Hospital Kharian	BBC reported it as the first SB attack in Punjab on an army training center.	
38	Political Gathering	District Hospital	Target Details: Federal Interior Minister Aftab Ahmad Sherpao	
39				
40	N/A	Lady Reading Hospital	According To Police That Restaurent Owner Sadruddin was An Uzbek Of Afghan Origin And He was a supporter OF Former Warlord Abdul Rashid Dostum.	
41		N/A		
42	N/A	Agency Headquarter Hospital		
43	N/A	N/A	Seventeen Rockets Were Fired On FC Fort In North Waziristan.	
44	N/A	Combined Military Hospital Banu		
45	N/A	N/A		
46	N/A	Saidu sharif Hospital		
47	N/A	Pims Hospital, Poly Clinic		
48	N/A	Combined Military Hospital Banu		
49	N/A	N/A		
50	N/A	N/A		

51	N/A	Combined Military Hospital Kohat	Interior Minister Aftab Sherpao Told AFP These Attacks Are A Backlash Reaction Against The Lal Masjid	
52	N/A	N/A		
53	N/A	pims Hospital, Poly Clinic, Capital Hospital		
54	N/A	N/A		
55	N/A	Government Hospital Parachinar		
56	N/A	N/A		
57	N/A	N/A		
58	N/A	N/A		
59	N/A	N/A		
60	N/A	N/A		
61	N/A	Bannu Hospital		
62	N/A	N/A		
63	Attack on a police van	N/A		
64	Checkpost targeted	N/A		
65	N/A	Agency Headquarters Hospital	No Group Has Claimed Responsibility For the Attack. But Telephone Calls To Local Journalists In Khar Asked Them To Report The Attack As Fidaee Hamla	
66	N/A	District Headquarters And Rawalpindi General Hospital		
67	N/A	N/A		
68	N/A	Dera Ismail Khan Headquarters Hospital		
69	N/A	Wapda Hospital CMH Attock And Rawalpindi		
70	N/A	N/A		

71	N/A	N/A		
72	N/A	Jinnah Hospital	Benazir Bhutto was Ex Prime Minister Of Pakistan She Was Returning From Self Exile After 8 Years	Miss Bhutto Was Threatened
73	N/A	Saidu sharif Hospital	SThe Army Announced That It Was Sending In 2500 Additional Troops To Swat To Maintain Law And Order, Fazlullah Warned In a Speech That His Supporters Would Retaliate If Security Forces Attacked them.	
74	N/A	District Headquarters Hospital, Combined Mil		
75	N/A	PAF Hospital And Combined Military Hospital		
76	N/A	Hayatabad Medical Complex		
77	N/A	N/A		
78	N/A	N/A		
79	N/A	N/A	It Was The First Time That Suicide Attacker Was Female	
80	N/A	N/A		
81	N/A	Combined Military Hospital Rawalpindi And PAF Kamra Hospital	The Suicide Attack Was On A School Which Was Carrying Air Force Employees Children	
82	N/A	Combined Military Hospital Quetta		
83	N/A	Combined Military Hospital Nowshera		
84	N/A	Combined Military Hospital Kohat		
85	Eid Ul Azha prayer	N/A		
86	N/A	N/A		
87	N/A	Rawalpindi General Hospital		

88	N/A	Civil Hospital Kabal		
89	N/A	Gangaram Hospital		
90	N/A	Ghalaanai Hospital		
91	N/A	Lady Reading Hospital		
92				
93	N/A	Mirali Headquarters Hospital		
94	N/A	Combined Military Hospital		
95	N/A	N/A	Suicide Bomber's Suicide Jacket Accidently Exploded	
96	N/A	Lady Reading Hospital		
97	N/A	N/A		
98	N/A	District Headquarters Saidu sharif		
99	N/A	Agency Headquarters Hospital		
100	N/A	Combined Military Hospital		
101	A Police Officers Funeral	Saidu sharif Hospital		
102	N/A	Agency Hospital Headquater Khar		
103	N/A	Lady Reading Hospital		
104	N/A	Combined Military Hospital		
105	N/A	Ganga Ram Hospital, Mayo Hospital		
106	N/A	N/A		
107	N/A	District Headquarters Saidu sharif		
108	N/A	Military Hospital		
109	N/A	N/A		

110	N/A	Combined Military Hospital Bannu	
111	N/A	Disrict Headquarters Hospital Saidu Sharif	
112	N/A	Combined Military Hospital & District Headquarters Hospital	
113	N/A	N/A	
114	N/A	PIMS &PolyClinic	
115	N/A	N/A	
116	Independence Day	Sheikh Zayed Hospital	
117	N/A	N/A	
118	N/A	P.O.F Hospital	
119	N/A	Lady Reading Hospital	
120	N/A	Saidu sharif Hospital	
121	N/A	Combined Military Hospital Kohat	
122	N/A	Lady Reading Hospital	
123	N/A	N/A	
124	Bombers blew themselves when hostage attempt was foiled	N/A	An attempt of taking 300 children hostage was foiled by residents and the bombers blew themselves	
125	N/A	C.D.A Hospital, Pims Hospital	
126	N/A	Combined Military Hospital Bannu	
127	N/A	N/A	
128	N/A	Combined Military Hospital	
129	Police Raid - one bomber blew himself	N/A	A handcuffed hostage was also killed.	
130	N/A	District Hospital Charsadda	

131	N/A	Nishtar Hospital District Hospital Bhakkar		
132	N/A	PIMS & PolyClinic		
133	N/A	N/A		
134	N/A	Kohat District Hospital		
135	N/A	N/A		
136	N/A	Ghalaanai Hospital		
137	N/A	N/A		
138	N/A	District Hospital Peshawar		
139	N/A	N/A		
140	N/A	Combined Military Hospital Thal		
141	N/A	N/A		
142	N/A	N/A		
143	N/A	N/A		
144	N/A	N/A		
145	N/A	N/A		
146	N/A	N/A		
147	Police patrol van targeted	N/A		
148	N/A	N/A		
149	N/A	N/A		
150	Local Fair	N/A		
151	Eid Ul Azha	N/A		
152	By Election	District Headquarter Hospital		
153	Checkpost targeted	N/A		
154	N/A	District Hospital D.I Khan		
155	N/A	N/A		
156	N/A	N/A		
157	N/A	District Headquarters Hospital & Nishtar Hospital		

158	N/A	N/A		
159	N/A	District Headquarters Hospital Bannu		
160	N/A	District Headquarters Hospital & Combined Military Hospital		
161	N/A	N/A		
162	N/A	N/A		
163	N/A	Civil Hospital Quetta		
164	N/A	Lady Reading Hospital		
165	N/A	District Headquarters Hospital & Combined Military Hospital		
166	N/A	N/A		
167	N/A	N/A		
168	N/A	Hayatabad Medical Complex & Lady Reading Hospital		
169	N/A	N/A		
170	Funeral Prayer of slain police official	N/A	Fateh Rehman's Funeral possession in dargai sub division	
171	N/A	PIMS & Polyclinic		
172	N/A	N/A		
173	N/A	District Hospital Chakwal & Rawalpindi		
174	N/A	District Hospital Charsadda & Peshawar		
175	N/A	Civil Hospital Hangu & Combined Military Hospital Thal		

176	N/A	Hayatabad Medical Complex		
177	N/A	District Hospital Peshawar & Kohat		
178	N/A	Combined Military Hospital Dera		
179	N/A	Mayo Hospital Services Hospital & Ganga Ram Hospital		
180	N/A	N/A		
181	N/A	N/A		
182	Juma Prayer	Hospitals In Upper Dir		
183	N/A	Pims Hospital		
184	N/A	Lady Reading Hospital		
185	N/A	Lady Reading Hospital		
186	N/A	Railway Cairns Hospital		
187	Juma Prayer	Hospitals In Nowshera & Peshawar		
188	N/A	N/A		
189	N/A	Combined Military Hospital Mazaffarabad	First Ever Suicide Attack In Azad Jammu Kashmir	
190	N/A	Agency Headquarters Hospital Landi Kotal		
191	N/A	N/A	First Ever Suicide Attack In Baloch Populated Area	
192	Police foiled an attempt, one militant blew himself	N/A		
193	N/A	Hospitals In Islamabad & Rawalpindi		
194	N/A	N/A		
195	N/A	N/A		
196	N/A	N/A		

197	N/A	N/A		
198	N/A	N/A		
199	N/A	N/A		
200	N/A	N/A		
201	N/A	Landi Kotal Hospital		
202	N/A	Saidu Sharif Hospital		
203	N/A	N/A		
204	N/A	N/A		
205	N/A	N/A		
206	N/A	Hospitals In Kohat	Most Of The Victoms Were Shia	
207	N/A	Hospitals In Peshawar		
208	Police foiled the assasination of education minster sardar hussain			
209	N/A	Lady Reading Hospital & Combined Military Hospital		
210	N/A	Hospitals In Bannu		
211	N/A	N/A		
212	N/A	Hospitals In Islamabad		
213	N/A	Lady Reading Hospital		
214	N/A	Alpuri Hospital		
215	N/A	District Hospital Kohat		
216	N/A	N/A		
217	N/A	Lady Reading Hospital		
218	N/A	Pims		
219	N/A	Hospitals In Kamra		
220	N/A	N/A		
221	N/A	District Hospital & Combined Military Hospital & Millitary Hospital	According To Eye Witnesses Many Of The Victoms Were Retired Military Personnel	

222	N/A	Mayo Hospital & Services Hospital		
223	N/A	Lady Reading Hospital		
224	N/A	Lady Reading Hospital		
225	N/A	Lady Reading Hospital & District Hospital Charsadda		
226	N/A	Lady Reading Hospital & Combined Military Hospital		
227	N/A	Hospitals In Bannu		
228	N/A	Lady Reading Hospital Hayatabad Medical Complex & Khyber Teaching Hospital		
229	N/A	Lady Reading Hospital		
230	N/A	Lady Reading Hospital		
231	N/A	N/A		
232	N/A	N/A		
233	Juma Prayer	Combined Military Hospital District Headquarters Hospital		
234	N/A	Services Hospital Mayo Hospital Sheikh Zaid Hospital		
235	N/A	Lady Reading Hospital		
236	N/A	Combined Military Hospital &Nishtar Hospital Civil Hospital		
237	N/A	District Hospital D.G Khan		
238	N/A	N/A		

239	N/A	Hospital In Peshawar & District Hospital Lower Dir		
240	N/A	Lady Reading Hospital	It was first Ever Suicide Attack On Journalists	
241	N/A	Hospitals In Peshawar		
242	Muharram Ul Haram	Pims		
243	Muharram Ul Haram	Hospitals In Muzaffarabad		
244	Muharram Ul Haram	Hospitals In Karachi		
245	N/A	Hospitals In Lakki Marwat		
246	N/A	Combined Military Hospital Rawalakot &Combined Military Hospital Rawalpindi		
247	N/A	N/A		
248	Bomber blew himself during police raid	N/A		
249	N/A	Combined Military Hospital Rawalakot		
250	N/A	Hospitals In Tank		
251	N/A	District Headquarters Hospital Khar & District Hospital Timargara		
252	N/A	Hayatabad Medical Complex & Hayatabad Teaching Hospital		
253	N/A	Hospitals In Bannu		
254	N/A	Hospitals In Kohat & Hangu		
255	N/A	District Headquarters Hospitals Mansehra		

256	N/A	Saidu Sharif Hospital & Combined Military Hospital Rawalpindi		
257	N/A	District Headquarters Hospitals Karak		
258	N/A	Combined Military Hospital Thal		
259	N/A	Jinnah Hospital General Hospital Shaikh Zayad Hospital		
260	N/A	N/A		
261	N/A	Services Hospital & General Hospital		
262	N/A	Saidu Sharif Hospital		
263	N/A	Agency Headquarters Hospital Khar		
264	N/A	N/A		
265	N/A	Khyber Teaching Hospital & Lady Reading Hospital		
266	N/A	Timergarah Hospital		
267	N/A	Civil Hospital Quetta & Combined Military Hospital	A Shia Doctor Was Killed When The Body Was Taken To The Hospital A Large Mob Was Present There When Suicide Bomber Blew Himself Up	
268	N/A	District Hospital Kohat & Liaqat Hospital	The IDPs Who Were Killed Mostly Shia	
269	N/A	District Headquarters Hospital		
270	N/A	Lady Reading Hospital & Al Khidmat Hospital		
271	N/A	Lady Reading Hospital		
272	N/A	Local Hospitals		

273	N/A	Hospitals In Lahore		
274	N/A	Mayo Hospital & Ganga Ram Hospital Services Hospital		
275	N/A	Lady Reading Hospital & Tehsil Headquarters Hospital Yakkaghund		
276	Malik Swab Khan's house targeted	N/A		
277	N/A	District Headquarters Hospital		
278	N/A	Lady Reading Hospital	People Were Gathered In And Outside Ministers House To Condole The Death Of His Son Rashid Who Was Gunned Down By Militants On Saturday	
279	N/A	Lady Reading Hospital		
280	N/A	Wana Hospital & Camp Hospital		
281	Anniversary Of Martyrdom Of Hazrat Ali (RZ)	Mayo Hospital Ganga Ram Hospital & Services Hospital		
282	Ahmedis Worship Place	N/A		
283	Quds Day	Civil Hospital Combined Military Hospital & Bolan Medical Complex		
284	N/A	Hospitals In Lakki Marwat		
285	N/A	Civil Hospital		
286	N/A	Jinnah Postgraduate Medical Center & Civil Hospital Karachi		

287	N/A	City Hospital		
288	N/A	Bacha Khan Medical Complex District Headquarters Hospital Swabi		
289	Juma Prayer	Lady Reading Hospital & Kohat District Hospital		
290	N/A	Jinnah Hospital & Civil Hospital		
291	N/A	Shaikh Zayad Hospital		
292	Busy Market place	N/A		
293	N/A	Hospitals In Bannu		
294	N/A	Lady Reading Hospital Headquarters Hospital Ghalanai		
295	N/A	Civil Hospital & Combined Military Hospital		
296	N/A	District Headquarters Hospital		
297	N/A	Civil Hospital Hangu		
298	N/A	Lady Reading Hospital & Combined Military Hospital		
299	N/A	N/A		
300	N/A	Hospitals In Khar & Peshawar	Suicide Bomber Was Woman	
301	N/A	ShaiKh Khalifa Bin Zayad Al Nahyan Hospital		
302	N/A	Hospitals In Bannu		
303	Chehlum Of Martyrs Of Karabla	Ganga Ram Hospital & Mayo Hospital		

304	Chehlum Of Martyrs Of Karabla	Jinnah Postgraduate Medical Center		
305	Militant blew himself when challenged at checkpost	N/A		
306	N/A	N/A		
307	N/A	Combined Military Hospital Mardan Combined Military Hospital Rawalpindi &Combined Military Hospital Peshawar		
308	N/A	N/A		
309	N/A	N/A		
310	N/A	Hospitals In Hangu		
311	N/A	Hospitals In Peshawar		
312	N/A	Combined Military Hospital Thall Hospitals In Hangu Hospitals In Doaba		
313	N/A	Hospitals In Swabi		
314	N/A	Hospitals In Charsadda & Hospitals In Peshawar	It Was Second Suicide Attack In Two Days On Fazal Ur Rehman A Religious Leader	
315	N/A	N/A		
316	N/A	District Headquarters Hospitals		
317	N/A	Timergarah Hospital		
318	N/A	Civil Hospital & Combined Military Hospital		
319	N/A	Tehsil Headquarter Hospital Khar		
320	N/A	Lady Reading Hosptal & Tehsil Hospital Shabqadar		

321	N/A	Local Hospitals	Five Dacoits Robbed A bank When They Came Out Of Bank People Reached There And Stopped them Meanwhile One Of Dacoit Blew Himself Up With Handgrenade	
322	N/A	Lady Reading Hosptal & Khyber Teaching Hospital		
323	N/A	District Headquarters Hospital		
324	N/A	District Headqaurters Hospital Khar Agency		
325	N/A	Lady Reading Hospital & Combined Military Hospital		
326	N/A	Lady Reading Hospital		
327	N/A	Pims	Disaster Averted By Guards Sacrifice Because He Did Not Let Him Enter The Bank	
328	N/A	Local Hospitals	Spokesman Confirmed That The Group Sent Two Attackers One Of Them Was A Woman	
329	N/A	Battagram District Headquarters Hospital		
330	N/A	N/A		
331	N/A	N/A	http://tribune.com.pk/story/216421/suicide-attack-on-checkpost-kills-one-security-personnel/	
332	Busy Market place	N/A		
333	A police van of Gulbahar police station	N/A		

334	Friday Prayer at Jamia Masjid Madina	N/A		
335	Eid ul Fitr prayer	N/A		
336	N/A	N/A		http://tribune.com.pk/story/243438/suicide-bomber-attacks-checkpost-in-lakki-marwat/
337	N/A	Civil Hospital & Combined Military Hospital	There Were Two Blasts One Was Packed In The Vehicle Carrying 100KG And Other With Suicide Jackets Was 15 To 20 Kg	
338	Funeral prayers in Jandol Town	N/A		
339	N/A	N/A		
340	N/A	N/A		
341	N/A	N/A		
342	Hi roof van of suspected terrorists blast on police post	N/A		
343	N/A	N/A		
344	N/A	N/A		
345	N/A	N/A	Residence of Shafiq Mengal, son of former chief minister and federa minister naseer mengal targeted	
346	N/A	N/A		
347	N/A	District Headquarters Hospital & Hospitals In Multan		
348	Bomber blew himself to avoid arrest	N/A		

349	N/A	Lady Reading hospital		
350	N/A	N/A		
351	Juma Prayer	Agency Headquarters Hospital		
352	N/A	N/A		
353	Juma Prayer	N/A		
354	N/A	Lady Reading Hospital		
355	N/A	District Headquarters Hospital		
356	Funeral Procession	Lady Reading Hospital		
357	N/A	Hayatabad Medical Complex & Khyber Teaching Hospital		
358	Juma Prayer	N/A	There Have Been A Series Of Conflicts Between Taliban And Lashkar e Islam In The Tribal Areas In Struggle For Influence In These Areas.	
359	N/A	N/A	Senior police officer, Anwar Ahmed Khan targeted	
360	N/A	Agency Headquarters Hospital Khar & Lady Reading Hospital		
361	N/A	N/A		
362	N/A	Lady Reading Hospital		
363	N/A	N/A		
364	N/A	Civil Hospital, Bolan Medical Complex	This Attack Was On The Bus Which was carrying Shia Pilgrims.	
365	N/A	Local Hospitals & Hospitals In Peshawar		
366	War between two militant outfits	N/A	4 children were killed (3 being girls)	
367	N/A	N/A		

368	N/A	N/A	http://www.dawn.com/news/743136/blast-near-security-forces-vehicle-kills-four-in-quetta	
369	N/A	Khyber Teaching Hospital		
370	N/A	Local Hospitals		
371	N/A	Lady Reading Hospital		
372	N/A	District Headquarters Hospital & Lady Reading Hospital		
373	N/A	Lady Reading Hospital		
374	N/A	Abbasi Shaheed Hospital & Sindh Rangers Hospital		
375	N/A	District Headquarters Hospital Ghalanai	Suicide Bomber Was A Woman	
376	Muharram Procession	Benazir Hospital & Holy Family Hospital		
377	Muharram Procession	District Headqaurters Teaching Hospital & Combined Military Hospital		
378	N/A	Tehsil Headquarter Hospital	But Mullah Nazir Survived A suicide Attack In Which 8 People Were Killed	
379	N/A	District Headquarters Hospital		
380	N/A	First Treatment Hospital & Scouts Hospital		
381	N/A	District Headquarters Hospital Bannu	http://www.thenews.com.pk/Todays-News-13-19386-Nine-killed-in-suicide-attack-on-Bannu-police-station	

382	Party Meeting	Lady Reading Hospital	Bashir Ahmed Bilour was killed in the attack as he was primary target.	http://tribune.com.pk/story/483051/peshawar-blast-kills-four-live-updates/
383	N/A	N/A		
384	N/A	Combined Military Hospital & Civil Hospital		
385	Friday Prayers	Lady Reading Hospital	The Blast Was For Shia Muslims But Sunni Muslims Also Died	
386	N/A	N/A		
387	N/A	N/A		
388	N/A	N/A		
389	While the police repulsed an attack	N/A		
390	N/A	N/A		
391	N/A	Combined Military Hospital & Bolan Medical Hospital	It Was For The First Time They Used Liquid Bomb	
392	House cum office of a PA attacked	N/A		
393	N/A	N/A		
394	N/A	N/A		
395	N/A	Lady Reading Hospital		
396	TTP headquarter attacked	NA		
397	N/A	N/A		
398	N/A	Lady Reading Hospital & Combined Military Hospital		
399	N/A	N/A		
400	N/A	N/A		

401	N/A	N/A		
402	N/A	N/A		
403	N/A	N/A		
404	N/A	N/A		
405	N/A	N/A		
406	Election Campaign	Local Hospitals		
407	N/A	N/A		
408	N/A	Local Hospitals		
409	N/A	Civil Hospital & Combined Military Hospital		
410	N/A	N/A		
411	N/A	N/A		
412	N/A	N/A		
413	N/A	N/A		
414	N/A	Local Hospitals		
415	N/A	N/A		
416	N/A	N/A		
417	N/A	Local Hospitals		
418	N/A	N/A		
419	Funeral Procession	Local Hospitals		
420	N/A	N/A		
421	N/A	N/A		
422	N/A	N/A		
423	N/A	N/A		
424	N/A	N/A		
425	N/A	N/A		
426	N/A	Local Hospitals		
427	N/A	Local Hospitals		
428	N/A	Local Hospitals		
429				
430	N/A	N/A		
431	N/A	Local Hospitals		
432	N/A	Local Hospitals		
433	N/A	Local Hospitals		

434	N/A	N/A	
435	N/A	N/A	
436	N/A	Local Hospitals	
437	N/A	Local Hospitals	
438	Funeral Procession	Local Hospital	They Were Offering Funeral Prayer Of A Police Officer Who Was Killed in Morning	
439	N/A	N/A	
440	N/A	N/A	
441	Sunday Services	Local Hospitals	
442	N/A	N/A	
443	N/A	Combined Military Hospital	
444	N/A	Combined Military Hospital Thall	
445	N/A	N/A	
446	N/A	N/A	
447	N/A	Local Hospitals	
448	N/A	Combined Military Hospital Bannu		http://www.geo.tv/article-126620-Four-troops-among-7-injured-in-Bannu-suicide-blast
449	N/A	N/A	The Motive Of The Attack Was Not Clear But In The Past Mlitant Groups Have Carried Out Suicide Attacks Against Each Other In The Tribal Belt.	http://www.dawn.com/news/1057360/ttp-commander-among-7-killed-in-suicide-attack
450	N/A	N/A	
451	N/A	N/A	
452	N/A	N/A	
453	N/A	Local Hospitals	
454	N/A	N/A	
455	N/A	Bolan Medical Hospital & Combined Military Hospital	

456	N/A	N/A	A teenager, aitazaz hassan was killed	
457	N/A	N/A		
458	Army possession			
459	N/A	Local Hospitals		
460	N/A	N/A		
461	N/A	JPMC		
462	N/A	Lady Reading Hospital		
463	During search operation by police	N/A		
464	N/A	Local Hospitals		
465	A bus carrying 50 police officers was targetted	N/A		
466	N/A	Local Hospitals	Only Suicide Bomber Died	
467	N/A	Local Hospitals		
468	N/A	Local Hospitals		
469	N/A	Lady Reading Hospital & Hayatabad Medical Complex		
470	N/A	N/A		
471	N/A	Local Hospitals		
472	N/A	Local Hospitals		
473	N/A	Local Hospitals		
474	N/A	N/A	One child was also killed	
475	N/A	Local Hospitals		
476	N/A	Lady Reading Hospital		
477	N/A	Combined MilitaryHospital, Bolan Medical Complex		
478	Jirga of the Zakhakhel Amn Lashkar	N/A		

479	N/A	Civil Hospital		
480	N/A	Local Hospitals		
481	N/A	Combined Military Hospital Lady Reading Hospital	The Number Of Attackers Were Not Confirmed	
482	N/A	N/A		
483	Juma Paryers	Civil Hospital Shikarpur		
484	Juma Paryers	Hospitals In Peshawar	There Were Three Suicide BombersOnly One Of Them Blew HimSelf Up	
485	N/A	Ganga Ram Hospital Mayo Hospital And Services Hospital		
486	Evening Prayer	N/A		
487	Sunday Prayers	Lahore General Hospital		
488	Routine Petrolling	N/A		http://www.topnewspk.com/suicide-blast-kills-two-rangers-personnel-in-karachi-59929.html